The Stars of Night

DEATH, men call thee hard
of heart and blind,
And weeping go
Railing at thee for ever;
but I know,
Death, thou art kind.

❋   ❋   ❋   ❋   ❋

The quiet of thy halls,
where is surcease
Of the world's gain,
Where is not any pleasure,
no, nor pain,
But only peace.

H.L.Simpson.O.
Carlisle.
February.19

Linda Hodgson and Sarah

British Library Cataloguing in Publication Data

A catalogue record for this book is available from the British Library

ISBN 978-0-9572412-8-2

Copyright © Linda Hodgson & Sarah Lee, 2014

Published in 2014 by:-

P3 Publications,13 Beaver Road, Carlisle, Cumbria, CA2 7PS.

Printed in Wales by:-

Gomer Press, Llandysul Enterprise Park, Ceredigion SA44 4JL.

Carlisle Grammar School and Trinity School

Readers not familiar with the history of the schools in Carlisle may wish to know how Trinity School originated from the Boys' Grammar School.

Prior to 1968 there were three schools on adjacent campuses along Strand Road in Carlisle, namely Carlisle Grammar School for boys, Creighton Secondary Modern School for boys and Margaret Sewell Secondary Modern School for girls.

In 1968 all of the schools in the city were amalgamated into Comprehensive schools. Trinity school was formed by the amalgamation of the three adjacent schools mentioned above, becoming at that time a 10 form entry comprehensive school.

Acknowledgements

This book would not have been possible without the support of the many family members of the Old Boys who have shared their family histories with us. In particular, Judith Carruthers (Henry Siviour Carruther's niece in law) assisted us in researching many of the families. We are also indebted to the many archivists, librarians and museum curators who have also provided photographs and other information. The Great War Forum members have been a valuable source of information. We have tried to obtain permission to use all our sources of information but if we have missed anyone, we beg forgiveness and ask that you contact us.

The students, staff and governors of Trinity School have been most encouraging; and the students who have accompanied us to the Great War battlefields have inspired us to discover as much as we can about these former students.

This book does not contain all our findings due to constraints of space, so please do visit our website www.trinity.cumbria.sch.uk/warmemorials, for more information and our source references. As several of our Boys joined the local regiment, we have been grateful to Col. HC Wylly's: *"The Border Regiment in the Great War"* for detailed information. We are indebted to John Kelly, the Web Developer at Trinity for his work on the website; to David Ramshaw who prepared the book for publication; and to Sarah's mother Monica Fyles-Lee who proofread the text.

Abbreviations

AWOL - Absent without Leave

BEF - British Expeditionary Force

CEF - Canadian Expeditionary Force

CGS - Carlisle Grammar School

CWGC - Commonwealth War Graves Commission

DLI - Durham Light Infantry

IWM - Imperial War Museum

NZEF - New Zealand Expeditionary Force

OTC – Officers Training Corps

RASC - Royal Army Service Corps

RFA - Royal Field Artillery

RFC - Royal Flying Corps – later the Royal Air Force

Foreword

423 students of the Carlisle Grammar School fought in the Great War of whom 90 were killed.*

These former students found themselves in all arenas of the war. They fought in the first battle of Ypres, at Passchendaele, at Arras, at Vimy Ridge, on the Somme, at Gallipoli and Salonika, in Mesopotamia, and at Jutland. While the majority died in the trenches of Belgium and France, some fell in Mesopotamia, or in Italy, Greece, Turkey, and India, and even one in Africa. Two died as prisoners-of-war, in Germany and Russia (now Latvia). The oldest casualty was 47, the youngest, 17. Some former students were professional soldiers; others joined up straight from school or university; while others left careers as teachers, engineers or journalists. Three men were in the Royal Flying Corps and three in the navy. There were six who died serving for Canada, two for Australia, and one for New Zealand. Many served as private soldiers, many as officers and some were awarded the Military Medal or the Croix de Guerre. However they lived and whatever the circumstances of their deaths, we hope – in this the Centenary year of the outbreak of the war – to fulfil the promise: *"We will remember them."*   **Linda Hodgson and Sarah Lee 2014**

*88 are on the original War Memorial. We have since discovered two more students and one teacher who also fell in the war.

The original War Memorial in the 'Old Hall' at Trinity School. (See page 135)

4

Robert Abram

DoB: September 21 1891

Regt: Border

CGS: 1904-11

DoD: October 26 1917

Age: 26

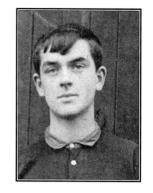

Commemorated: Tyne Cot Memorial, Belgium

Robert was the second child of seven born to Thomas (a locomotive engine driver) and Mary Jane Abram and only he and younger brother Henry attended the Grammar School.

Robert was good at sport at school: he captained the Rugby XV in 1910 having played in the team in 1908 and 1909 *("The hardest worker in the scrum, and one of the keenest at practices. With a little more originality in the open he would become a really good forward.")*. As Captain he was described as *"energetic"* in the school magazine.

He was academic: winning form prize in 1908; and prizes for English, Greek and Geography in 1909. In 1911 the School Medal for good character and proficiency was awarded to him. He was also a keen member of the debating society. One of the debates in 1909 concerned whether Britain should fear a German invasion. Robert thought not. He preferred football to cricket; town life to country; and was against aviation! In 1911 he spoke against women's suffrage; and military conscription!

Robert was killed in the Battle of Passchendaele. October 26 had been a day of heavy losses for the Border Regiment and Captain Abram's death is reported in Col Wylly's account of the Regiment in the Great War: *"the men got stuck in mud up to their waists and were almost entirely wiped out by machine-gun fire"; "Practically the whole of this company fell..."*

Reginald John Atkinson

DoB: January 3 1898

Regt: Liverpool

CGS: 1914-16

DoD: June 3 1917

Age: 19

Buried: Cite Bonjean Military Cemetery, Armentieres, France

Reginald John Atkinson was born at Bowness-on-Solway, a small fishing/farming community, some twelve miles west of Carlisle. His father Thomas was the local schoolmaster. Reginald was the youngest of Thomas and Mary's five children. When Reginald was six months old his brother Thomas died in an outbreak of measles. Thomas and Mary had married at Darlington in 1881, Thomas's family were from County Durham and Mary's from Manfield, Yorkshire. They moved to the Bowness area when Thomas was appointed Headteacher of Anthorn School and later at Bowness School so they moved to the village and lived there for over thirty years. Thomas was a meticulous keeper of school records and even records the death of his son. He shut the school for several days when Reginald died.Teaching was part of the Atkinson family's way of life, Reginald planned to be a teacher and his sisters and brother Gerald also taught. Gerald was in Canada when war broke out and he enlisted in the CEF, and survived the war.

Reginald and Gerald both attended Carlisle Grammar School. Reginald then remained at the Grammar School in the Pupil Teacher's Class, gaining teaching experience as a pupil teacher at Bowness, and Burgh by Sands Schools; he finally left the Grammar School in July 1916. He had completed his pupil teacher course, passing the Senior Cambridge Local Examination, thus qualifying for college. However he enlisted instead of going to college.

Reginald enlisted in October 1916 and went to London. Writing to his sister Mabel that he was not impressed by the big city and commenting on how dirty it was. He also ran out of money and asked her to send him some!

He was killed on sentry duty in a front line trench, on June 3 1917. A letter written by one of his comrades to Reginald's parents was quoted in his obituary in The Cumberland News (16 June 1917)

"We have lost a good soldier and a good pal. Reg. was well liked by all the boys and was a good Lewis gunner."

Tragedy was to follow in the family as Reginald's nephew, Thomas Geoffrey Atkinson, died aged 20 in 1944. He was a flying officer in the RAF and he is buried at Bari, Italy.

Reginald is also commemorated on the Bowness-on-Solway War Memorial and on the memorial plaque in the church, as well as in Armentieres.

An Atkinson family group photograph.

George Newell Ballantine

DoB: August 14 1894

Regt: Manchester

CGS: 1903-9

DoD: August 7 1915

Age: 20

Helles Memorial Turkey

Commemorated: Helles Memorial, Turkey

George Newell Ballantine was one of five children born to William Newell Ballantine and Minnie (née Carr). His three brothers died aged two, three and nine years old, leaving his parents with George and his sister Minnie. She became a teacher and died unmarried aged nearly 80. The Ballantine and Carr families lived near each other at Higher Bebington, Cheshire in 1881, William and Minnie married in 1884. His father had started his working life as a painter and decorator and then became a commercial traveller selling paint. His father's family had come from London and his grandfather had been a decorator too. His paternal grandmother was Charlotte Rebecca Newell, born in Ireland. His mother came from a large family which had finally settled in Cheshire, although his mother was born in Liverpool and her parents were from Yorkshire and Edinburgh.

George's maternal grandfather was the most famous member of the family. He was a copperplate engraver by trade, but his passion was bee-keeping and he was invited by Thomas William Cowan to go to London and help set up and edit *The Beekeeper's Journal*. In 1890 he invented a type of beehive which is known as the *WBC*. He wrote articles on bees for the 1911 edition of the *Encyclopaedia Britannica* but died before they were published.

At the grammar school George was a day student. He must have had one of the shortest walks to school as the family lived on Howard Place. He won the French and Latin prizes in 1908.

After leaving school George became a manufacturing chemist's assistant, but by 1911 he was working as an insurance clerk.

The Territorial Force was formed in 1908 and George was recruit number 1491 which suggests that he enlisted prior to war breaking out, he was probably a *"Saturday afternoon soldier"*. The 6th Manchester regiment was sent to Egypt in September 1914 where a great deal of basic training took place. Allied forces first landed on the Gallipoli Peninsula in April 1915. The Regiment moved to Gallipoli in May. In August the Battle of Krithia Vineyard took place to divert attention from a planned landing at Suvla. Between August 7 and 9 there was a series of attacks with little ground gained. There were at least 4000 British casualties, and probably double that number of Ottoman casualties. On August 7 the regiment's war diary notes that 140 men were dead, wounded or missing. Later records say that a minimum of seventy-five men were killed including George. His body was never found; he died a week before his twenty-first birthday.

Carlisle C of E Grammar School
(early 20th Century photograph)

Bertie Bowman Barton

DoB: February 10 1884

Regt: King's Royal Rifle Corps

CGS: 1893-8

DoD: November 30 1917

British Mark V First World War tank

Age: 33

Commemorated: Cambrai Memorial, France

Bertie Bowman Barton was born just 366 days after his only sibling Henry. They were the sons of Thomas Barton and Martha (née Bowman). Thomas was brought up at 1 The Crescent, Carlisle, where the family firm was located behind the house. In 1881 he was there aged 48, living with his widowed mother, probably with everyone assuming that he was a confirmed bachelor! In just under three years by February 10 1884, he was married and the father of two sons. In 1893 Thomas died and the boys were under the guardianship of their bachelor uncle Robert. The Bartons were a fairly wealthy Carlisle family. Thomas and Robert are listed as coach builders on all census returns up to 1891, and their father had started the business. They built horse-drawn coaches and then went on to train coaches. The National Railway Museum in York has one of their coaches. Robert sold the business as a going concern sometime after Thomas died. Robert died in early 1917 and left his considerable fortune to Bertie whose mother came from Newcastle, where her father had had a printing business, but it seems to have been on a smaller scale than the Bartons' business. She was nearly twenty years younger than her husband. No trace of her can be found after the 1891 census.

Bertie and his elder brother Henry both attended the Grammar School and then Fettes College, Edinburgh. Bertie then went to Trinity Hall Cambridge, graduating with a B.A. in 1908, becoming a barrister.

He married Gertrude Frances Crofts Pearson on December 9 1909 at St. Georges's Hanover Square, London. In 1911 they were living in Windsor Mansions, in London, Bertie described himself as a law student.

Bertie was a conscript, called up under the Military Services Acts of 1916. He had enlisted into the Inns of Court Officer Training Corps on October 1 1914 but had been discharged on November 4 1914 due to "*unsatisfactory conduct*"! Bertie was firstly in the Rifle Brigade as a private, then he was promoted to Lance Corporal and went to the 10th King's Royal Rifle Corps. He was reported missing in the Battle of Cambrai on November 30 1917, one of the first battles which included tanks.

Gertrude inherited nearly £20,000 as Bertie had inherited so much money from his uncle earlier that year. Gertrude died in 1962, never having remarried. She was still putting memorial notices for Bertie in newspapers in 1941.

The main entrance to the modern Trinity School which has retained the original facade of the old Margaret Sewell Secondary Modern School building.

11

James Herbert Batey

DoB: November 6 1893

Regt: Gordon Highlanders

CGS: 1907-8

DoD: May 16 1915

Age: 21

Commemorated: Le Touret Memorial, France

A. McCULLOCH
J. H. BATEY
W. McKENZIE
M. McKENZIE

J H Batey commemorated on the Longtown Memorial. See page 20.

James was one of 13 children born to James and Elizabeth Batey, a well known Longtown family who had a game dealer's business at 37, English Street for many years. James joined the family business after leaving school.

James had probably won a scholarship to the Grammar School. At school he was a gymnast and played centre forward in the football team. The end of season report described him as *"a useful player, unselfish and fast"* he scored seven goals during the season. Two of James's brothers also attended CGS.

James enlisted at Dumfries, joining the 2nd Battalion Gordon Highlanders on January 11 1915. He was 5ft 7" tall, and weighed 11 stone. He embarked at Southampton on March 24 1915, having been made acting corporal on March 9. He was killed in action just 52 days after leaving Southampton. He died in the battle for Festubert and is commemorated on the memorial at Le Touret, in France; and is one of the 13,394 men who died in that area who have no known grave. He is also commemorated on Longtown War Memorial and on his parents' headstone in Arthuret Churchyard.

His obituary in the Cumberland News (29/5/1915) says *"He was a strong well built lad and a type of the British soldier keen at all kinds of sport, and held in the greatest esteem by all who knew him."*

Richard Beeby

DoB: June 14 1891

Regt: AIF

CGS: 1904-7

DoD: May 9 1918

Age: 26

Ebblinghem Military Cemetery, France.

Buried: Ebblinghem Military Cemetery, France

Richard was the elder son of Richard and Jane Alice Beeby (née Johnston), both of Carlisle. His father was a commercial clerk and his mother was the daughter of a builder. Brother John went on to serve with the Border Regiment in India.

When Richard joined up in May 1916 he was described as a railway porter. He was a man of average height, 5'7", fair, with blue eyes. On the form he said he had previously been in the army. This is possibly borne out by a letter from an Australian, R Beeby, to the Cumberland News published on 9 October 1915 where he says he is a "Carlisle man" and is looking for pals in the North. He said he was in the Dardanelles for 15 weeks and had been in King George's Hospital for eight weeks *"with a piece of bomb in the eye and concussion".*

Having joined up again in 1916, he left Sydney in September 1916 travelling to England before being posted to France. He had some trouble adjusting to soldiering it seems. He went AWOL for three days in January 1917. He lost 10 days' pay and received 168 hours detention.

Richard was wounded in May and was hospitalised in France and was then transferred to hospital in England for a month. On the casualty form he was listed as a Gunner in the 1st Battalion Light Trench Mortar Battery. In February 1918 in France he was in trouble again, being reprimanded for being improperly dressed, and in town without a pass. He was wounded in action in May and died of his wounds.

Francis Richard Lowry Bell

DoB: August 27 1891

Regt: Border

CGS: 1904-9

DoD: Feb 23 1916

Age: 24

Buried: Norfolk Cemetery, Becordel-Becourt, France

Francis was born six weeks before the death of his father after whom he was named. His mother, Elizabeth (née Johnson) was 27 and also had a daughter Annie Mary, aged two. Francis's parents had married at Arthuret Church, Longtown in 1887 as Elizabeth's family farmed in the area. Francis was from Hesket in the Forest where his family had farmed for three generations.

Francis was a day pupil at the Grammar School where he was a member of the Debating Society and he also won the bicycle race on sports day. On leaving school Francis joined the firm of J M Richardson & Son, and then the Land Valuation Dept. of the Inland Revenue, and later Messers Frank and Rutley, of Edinburgh.

Francis joined the Border Regiment, and was given a commission as 2nd Lieutenant. The action in February 1916 is described by Wylly thus:

"In February it (the battalion) was in the trenches near Meaulte, where there were many casualties, especially from shell fire, casualties which the small, if frequent, drafts which arrived at the front were hardly adequate to replace."

Francis's obituary in the Cumberland News says:

"Lieutenant Bell who was attached to the 2nd Border Regiment, had only been in the trenches two or three days when he was struck by shrapnel and killed. He was a young man of great promise, only 24 years of age".

George Bott

DoB: September 30 1886

Regt: Rifle Brigade

CGS: 1897-1906

DoD: February 9 1917

Age: 30

Buried: Philosophe British Cemetery, France

Thanks to the Bott family for the photograph

George was the eldest of twelve children of the Rev. Richard Bott and his wife Sarah Faulder. In 1901 George was boarding at Carlisle Grammar School. He took an active part in school sporting activities and he was a member of the debating society. He became a prefect and head of school.

After school, George studied at St Edmund Hall, Oxford, became a tutor and seemed intent on taking Holy Orders like his father. The war intervened however, and George enlisted instead in the Public Schools Battalion of the Royal Fusiliers on September 2 1914. He served in the ranks of the BEF in France between November 1915 and March 1916 and was then commissioned as 2nd Lieutenant, in the 3rd Rifle Brigade. He returned to France in September 1916. His B.A. degree was conferred in his absence, on December 16 1916.

George was killed in action near Loos in February 1917. His Commanding Officer wrote: *"He was justly regarded as one of the most efficient officers of his Battalion. He had won the very greatest personal popularity with both officers and men and his men would have followed him anywhere."* A brother officer wrote: *"He was absolutely fearless. All the little jobs that no one has to do and yet are everyone's job always found him willing. He was always ready to work for the success of others."* His servant wrote: *"I have been in France since the war began and I have never met a better friend and soldier in an officer. He was everything in the way of cheerfulness and for helping others. His platoon miss him very much."*

Alastair Bruce Bremner

Dob: May 27 1884

Regt: N. Rhodesian Police

CGS: 1893-6

Dod: January 1 1918

Age: 33

Buried: Ndola (Kansenshi) Cemetery, Zambia

Alastair was the younger son of William Bremner and Diana Harriet Bruce. His maternal grandfather was Major General Alexander James Bruce of the Madras Staff Corps. His parents were both born in the East Indies. This was clearly a background of Colonial Service and Empire. He had an older sister, Helen Marianne and a brother, Huntley William Bruce, who was killed on the Somme on July 1 1916. He also features on the Carlisle Grammar School War Memorial.

The police force of Rhodesia, was for the most part, the British South Africa Police (BSAP). It was formed in 1889 by Cecil Rhodes' British South Africa Company, as a paramilitary force of mounted infantrymen. It began to operate independently in 1896 and then served as Rhodesia's regular police force. Alastair was in the Northern Rhodesia Police and aged 33 when he died, the result of an accident. The Bulawayo Chronicle of January 11 1918 reported that Captain Bruce had been seeing off some native askari troops at the station and his horse had been troublesome, then as he: *"remounted to return home, the horse bolted before he was fairly in the saddle and he was not able to get his off foot in the stirrup at all. When just beyond the Headquarters Stores, the horse suddenly swerved, throwing the Captain into a tree. He was at once... taken in a sidecar to the hospital, but he never regained consciousness...Death was due to internal haemorrhage caused by five fractured ribs and a broken sternum...He was accorded a funeral with full military honours...Captain Bremner was a young and popular officer...".*

Huntley William Bruce Bremner

DoB: September 21 1880

Regt: London

Carlisle Grammar School: 1889-6

DoD: July 1 1916

Age: 35

Stretcher bearers, Battle of Thriepval Ridge.

Commemorated: Thiepval Memorial, France

Huntley was the elder son of William Bremner and Diana Harriet Bruce. His maternal grandfather was Major General Alexander James Bruce of the Madras Staff Corps. His parents were both born in the East Indies: giving Huntley a background of Colonial Service and Empire. He was born in Edinburgh, but in the 1891 Census the family was living at Portland Square, Carlisle. He had a younger sister, Helen Marianne and a brother, Alastair Bruce, who was a Captain in the Great War and died in Livingstone, Rhodesia (Zambia) in 1918. He also features on the Carlisle Grammar School War Memorial.

Huntley joined up in January 1916, having returned from Ceylon (Sri Lanka) in October 1915. He had first gone there in 1902 to be a tea planter and presumably returned in order to join up. He joined the 14th Battalion of the London Regiment, which was known as *"The London Scottish"*. He served in France from June and was reported missing on July 1 1916 and was afterwards reported killed on that date. De Ruvigny's Roll of Honour reports: *"He was a well-known athlete."*

17

James Robert Caird

DoB: November 4 1892

Regt: King's Own Scottish Borderers

CGS: 1901-11

DoD: April 23 1915

Age: 22

Commemorated: Menin Gate, Belgium

James Robert Caird was born in India in 1892; the son of a professional soldier and grandson of an MP and Scottish landowner. By the 1901 Census James was living with step-mother and siblings in Bedford but father was a Major in the Border Regiment at Carlisle Castle. Presumably this was why young James came to the Grammar School in Carlisle.

James seems to have been good at sport as he played in the Rugby team. He also played fives and cricket; he swam and he came first in the sack race on sports' day. He was a key member of the debating society. In – what appears to have been a tongue in cheek debate on alcohol – James spoke in favour of brandy and said that wine did *"people a great deal of good"*. He liked drama and appeared in performances of "A Midsummer Night's Dream" and "Much Ado about Nothing". In his final year he won prizes for geography and divinity.

James was a member of the Inns of Court O.T.C. when war broke out. He obtained a commission in 3rd King's Own Scottish Borderers, August 15, 1914 and served with 2nd Bn. Highland Light Infantry near Ypres, from November 1914, to March, 1915. He took part in the capture of Hill 60. He was only 22 when he died on April 23 1915, during the advance on St Julien. A witness, a Sergeant McMurchy reported he was shot through the head and died instantly. James had applied for a permanent commission – clearly he intended to be a career soldier like his father. One sad postscript is a letter in 1920 from his father concerning the 1914-5 Star to which his son was entitled.

Robert Mayson Calvert

DoB: March 1 1896

Regt: Manchester

CGS: 1903-10

DoD: July 9 1916

Age: 20

Buried: Serre Road Cemetery, No2, France

R.M.CALVERT

Robert was the youngest of four children born to Robert and Fanny Maria (née Blaylock). His father Robert was a sea captain. Both families the Blaylocks and Calverts were Cumbrian, the Blaylocks had farmed in the Burgh by Sands area for generations. With Robert away at sea so much it is not surprising that Fanny and the children lived at Burgh by Sands so that she could have the support of her family.

Robert was very academic he won the school Latin and French prizes three years running. He also came 2nd in the 100 yd dash. He won a scholarship to St.Bees School, and then went as a Hastings Exhibitioner, to Queen's College, Oxford.

He was appointed to be temporary Second Lieutenant in the 17th Battalion of The Manchester Regiment on April 8 1915. He had asked to join the Manchester Regt. In March 1916 he joined his regiment in France and died three months later in the battle for Trones Wood. The Battalion had received orders the night before to attack at 5.30am, which they did. The War Diary is very detailed, they did not enter the wood until 6.40am, and there was "fearful shelling"; they were forced to withdraw at 3pm because of their losses, 196 ordinary ranks and 10 officers died that day.

His father Robert wrote to the War Office asking about "the manner of his death"; the reply stated that Rupert Carline also of the 17th Manchester Regt had reported from his bed in Killingbeck Hospital Leeds, that *"on the 9th July* at Trones Wood, he'd seen Lieutenant Calvert lying dead on the field". In the War Diary Box at the National Archives there is a small sheet of paper with a list of casualties on it, next to Robert's name it says "before Trones Wood", so it seems likely that he died early in the attack before they left the fields and entered the wood. His Obituary in St. Bees School Roll of Honour confirms this it says *"He was killed leading his men into action on July 9, 1916, when the battalion attacked and took Trones Wood."*

From the diary of Lt Kenneth MacArdle (held at IWM) - *" Calvert – a student of classics lately from St Bees in Cumberland, with bored looking wrinkles on his forehead and an inability to pronounce his "R"s which he substitutes with "W"s. He was meant for the Civil Service but makes a good enough soldier and is as comic as a clown with a tired resentful expression."*

Robert has a brass memorial plaque in the parish church at Burgh-by-Sands, it is next to the memorial dedicated to his great grandparents George and Elizabeth Blaylock. It reads

"To the beloved memory of Robert Mayson Calvert, 2nd Lieutenant 17th Manchester Regt. Hastings Exhibition at Queen's College Oxford, youngest son of Robert Calvert of Burgh by Sands b 1.Mar 1896 killed in action in Trones Wood France, 9th July 1916 during the battle of the Somme"

Robert's second cousin, George Norman, is also commemorated on the CGS memorial, he too was a great-grandson of George and Elizabeth Blaylock.

Thiepval July 2013 with our Guide Simon Barber.

John Santiago Campbell

Dob: July 15 1891

Regt: Argyll and Sutherland Highlanders

CGS: 1904-7

DoD: September 28 1917

Age: 26

Buried: Pont du Hem Military Cemetery, France

John Santiago was the eldest son of Archibald Jack Campbell and his wife Catherine Crawford. He was born in Spain as his father was working in a shipyard near Bilbao. Both of his parents came from the Glasgow area. His maternal grandfather was a shipyard manager and his paternal grandfather is variously described as a foreman blacksmith and shipsmith. Archibald was born in Govan and had worked in J & G Thomson's drawing office in the Clydebank Shipyard before going to work in Spain. When he married Catherine in 1889 he gave Spain as his home address. He was very successful in Spain and was awarded the Cruz de Merito, Naval.

The young family moved to Barrow-in-Furness when Archibald got a job at Vickers Naval Construction Works. The Vickers company was at the forefront of airship design and construction. At least five more children were born 1893-1906. In about 1912 the family moved back to the Glasgow area when Archibald became general manager of William Beardmore & Company's Dalmuir Naval Construction Works, which was also involved with airships.

John was a boarder at school and was also an active member of the debating society speaking against the motion *"That the Press has more power than the pulpit"*

And in the debate *"That War is Justifiable"*, the *Carliol* magazine reports that: *"He avowed that war was but a carnal instinct, and, as such, better fitted for beasts than men"*

21

In his final year he presented a book to the library *"True to His Colours"* by the Rev.Theodore P. Wilson.

John enlisted on October 29 1914 as a second lieutenant in the 9th battalion of Princess Louise's Argyll and Sutherland Highlanders. He must have then volunteered for the newly created Royal Flying Corps. In November 1916 he was wounded in a flying accident whilst still in the UK. In May 1917 he graduated as a flying officer, was posted to 82 squadron and promoted to lieutenant. He was then sent to learn how to fly Bristol F2B two seat fighters. In August 1917 he was promoted to captain and on September 1 was posted to 20 Squadron in France.

On September 28, John's plane was one of eight Bristols sent up to photograph German troops and positions. They were attacked by 25 albatros aircraft and John's plane was last seen in combat near Menin. John and his observer George Tester were declared missing in action the next day. They had been shot down and buried by the Germans. It was some months before their deaths were officially confirmed. In 1924 the CWGC exhumed their bodies and reburied them at Pont du Hem, France.

Bristol F2B two seat fighter

Lawrence Stanley Carrick

DoB: June 26 1882

Regt: Canadian Infantry Battalion

CGS: 1892-6

DoD: September 15 1916

Age: 34

Commemorated: Vimy Memorial, France

Lawrence Stanley Carrick was the youngest of eight children born to John and Catherine Elizabeth Carrick. His father who was a solicitor died when Lawrence was eight years old. The family seem to have been left well provided for.

After leaving the Grammar School Lawrence went to Rugby School. He must have had an adventurous nature as he went to South Africa and joined the East Griqualand Mounted Rifles, and fought in the last year of the Second Boer War. Lawrence next went to Canada to join his brother John William farming. He then joined the Canadian Light Horse, and the North West Mounted Police. After war broke out he enlisted on September 23 1914, joined 19th Alberta Dragoons and was sent to Europe with the first Canadian contingent.

On his enlistment he is described as 5ft 5 ½ inches tall with fair hair and a medium complexion. He had a tiger's head tattoo on his right forearm.

He was shot through the head by a sniper at 8am on September 15 1915, one of 128 members of the 49th Canadian Infantry Battalion who died that day. His body was not recovered for burial and he is commemorated on the Vimy Memorial. Although his body was never identified his obituary in the Cumberland News states that he died just twenty yards from the German front. Later in the long obituary it quotes a letter from a brother officer *"He was a most capable officer and genial companion, and beloved by everybody".*

Henry Siviour Carruthers

DoB: January 10 1897

Regt: London

CGS: 1909-12

DoD: April 6 1917

Age: 20

Buried: Nikolai Cemetery, Latvia

Henry Siviour Carruthers was the elder son of Joseph and Margaret Carruthers Joseph was a grocer; and Henry and his adopted brother, Ralph were brought up over the shop on Rickergate.

Henry and his brother both attended the Grammar School, had minor County Council Scholarships and were day students.

When he was 15 in 1912 Henry was accepted as a boy clerk for the GPO a post of responsibility in West Kensington, London. He joined the London Regiment.

The Cumberland published news of Henry on July 3 1915 under the heading

"CARLISLE PRISONER OF WAR", it read

"Rifleman H.T. Carruthers, of the 12th County of London Regiment (The Rangers), son of Mr Joseph Carruthers, Richergate who has been missing since May 8th has written to say he was slightly wounded at Ypres and taken prisoner. He was kindly treated while in hospital and is POW in camp in Germany".

Henry died on April 6 1917 as a German prisoner of war, in modern day Latvia and is buried at Nikolai, one of 32 graves. The conditions in the POW camp were appalling, Henry starved to death. The following are excerpts taken from a précis of a statement by Company Sergeant-Major A. Gibb, 2nd Argyll and Sutherland Highlanders.

"*No. 4 Company to which the statement refers was employed in the docks in LIBAU from 14th May 1916 to February 1917. On 23rd February the company, strength 500 left LIBAU for MITAU, AND ON THE 25th marched along the frozen River Aa to the village of LATCHEN, NEAR KELZIEN, a distance of 25 kilometres. The escort of the party, a squadron of Uhlans, drove the party along all day in the most brutal manner possible, and only about 80 of the 500 were able to reach LATCHEN in any sort of formation.*

Accommodation at the new camp was one tent, about 70 yards by 7, for all the 500 N.C.O's and men, pitched on a frozen swamp. No fuel for heating the tent, no light, no proper means of obtaining water for cooking or washing, and rations barely sufficient to keep the men alive. Orders were read, stating that the British had been brought to this place as a reprisal for the employment of Germans in France, where they were being ill-treated, starved and made to work under fire. The orders to the guard stated that no mercy was to be shown to the prisoners, every one of whom had assisted to stop the Kaiser's army from reaching Paris. The treatment was so brutal that the men soon became mere living skeletons, too weak to move about. Nevertheless, they were kicked and beaten out to work morning after morning by the medical feld-webel; their comrades had to help them to walk out, lead them about all day and very often carry them home at night. Hospital accommodation was quite inadequate in the camp and medical comforts or attention almost non-existent. The result, in figures, was that 14 men died at the camp, and eight more in hospital at MITAU, all from exhaustion and starvation except one who was murdered".

Private Skett was shot by a German sentry when he collapsed from exhaustion.

"*Private Carruthers, 12th London Regiment, who had also been left in that morning too weak to go out and work, died during the 6th April. His body was placed beside that of Private Skett and both covered with a sheet of tin. I buried them both on the morning of the 9th about 100 yards from the hut. They were both simply human skeletons*"

Stanley Campbell Cheverton (Smith)

DoB: March 22 1896

Regt: Border

CGS: 1905-09

DoD: January 27 1917

Age: 20

Buried: Quarry Cemetery Montauban, France

Thanks to the Cheverton family for the photograph

Stanley Campbell Cheverton was born Stanley Campbell Smith, son of Captain Francis John Smith and Clarissa Mary Campbell, in South Africa in 1896. His older brother Francis Penn (who served in India during both world wars) had similarly been born in Cape Town three years earlier, although younger siblings Reginald and Lorna were born in Kent and Carlisle respectively. Their father was a soldier and rose to the rank of Lieutenant Colonel and was later an army chaplain who also served in the Great War. The family changed its name in 1905 to Cheverton.

Stanley was a keen musician and played the organ at Carlisle Cathedral. He joined the Public School Brigade, Royal Fusiliers, at the age of 18 and went to Sandhurst Officer Cadet College. In May 1915 he was commissioned into the Border Regiment and joined the 1st Battalion on October 10 1915 at Gallipoli. He suffered from shell shock and was sent *"sick to hospital"* at Suez in Egypt whilst en route to France in January 1916, though by February he was reported as proceeding to Ismalia for training on the Lewis machine gun. He re-joined the regiment in France, from leave in England, in October 1916 and on January 12 1917 he moved up from base to join the Regiment at the front.

The Battalion had rested at Carnoy on January 23, practising assaults for the next two days. On January 26 they moved up to the firing line and Stanley had supper with his brother Frank. It was to be their last meeting as Stanley was killed during an early morning raid on Le Transloy road on the Somme. The attack had begun at 5.30am and the first objective was gained, and the first prisoners taken, by 7.15am. Success continued through the morning, despite the frozen ground, and by the afternoon it was reported in the Battalion War Diary that:" *All objectives gained and consolidation proceeding very slowly owing to hardness of ground"*. Stanley's commanding officer said *"He led his platoon most gallantly across No Man's Land right up to the enemy's wire. By his careful handling and keeping his men close up to our barrage our casualties amongst the men were very slight"*. Stanley however was one of the officers killed. He was buried in the area with a wooden cross to mark the spot.

In December 1918 Stanley's father applied for his medals. In 1919 Stanley's body was reinterred at the Quarry War Graves Cemetery, at Montauban, east of Albert. His father and younger brother attended and took photographs of the grave and the site.

Thanks to the Cheverton family for the photograph

The Cheverton Family   taken on 29 December 1916

Stanley Campbell   Reginald   Clarissa (mother)   Francis (father)   Frank

Lorna

John Asheton Critchley

DoB: November 4 1892

Regt: Lord Strathcona Horse (Canada)

CGS: 1904-06

DoD: April 5 1917

Age: 24

Buried: Bray Cemetery, France

John Asheton Critchley (Jack) was the son of Oswald Asheton Critchley and his wife Mary Winifred Holt. His father had been married before and had two sons, Alfred Cecil, and Walter Ramsay, with his first wife, Maria Cecil Newbold who died in childbirth in 1891. In 1905 Jack's twin brothers Gerald Holt and Richard Oswald were born. The family lived at the Stapleton Ranch which was six miles west of Calgary: *"it was all most picturesque: some of the mountain peaks carried white caps of snow all the year round"* and his half-brother Alfred recalled: *"Walter, Jack…and I were growing up without the slightest benefit of education. We could hardly write and could only just read. On the other hand, we could saddle ponies, ride for miles across the ranges, find our way in the dark without compasses, make our own camp, hit a polo ball, and ride herd."*

The family moved to England in 1899 for the boys' education. This was why Jack ended up at Carlisle Grammar School and then at St Bees.

Alfred joined Lord Strathcona Horse first: *"Later in 1911 my younger half-brother Jack joined us. He stood 6ft.4in. and was one of the finest horsemen I have ever known….There are few more pleasant lives than that of a subaltern in a cavalry, if you like horses, but it was fairly strenuous; up at 5a.m. in the summer for stables and 6a.m. in the winter, and then you were kept hard at it till lunch. In the afternoon there were drills and sport, followed by evening stables."* Jack, along with Alfred, was on the polo team for Strathcona's.

In October 1914 33,000 men and 7 000 horses sailed to England. In May they went to France. They went as infantry and were asked to volunteer as they were cavalry trained: "there was not a single man who did not volunteer". (From "Always a Strathcona" by W.B. Fraser) On May 22nd, the Regiment was moving up near Festubert when they met up with Captain Walter Critchley of 10th Canadian Battalion who was to escort them. W.B. Fraser reports: *"The situation was rather unique. Captain Critchley's father Lieutenant O.A. Critchley, was machine gun officer with Lord Strathcona's Horse; a brother, Captain A.C. Critchley, was Regimental Adjutant; while another brother, Lieutenant J.A. Critchley, was senior subaltern. Briefly the father and three sons were brought together on the battlefield."* The following account is taken from Alfred's autobiography: *"The Germans promptly attacked. They seemed to have a disconcerting amount of information about what was going on. Their attack was really quite exciting to us, but discipline was good, and we had no trouble in holding the Germans off. In fact, my brother Jack was so annoyed at being attacked before he got settled in that he took his troop over the top and chased the Germans all the way back to their own lines. This so surprised them that Jack emerged with practically no losses at all, and actually picked up a Military Cross within a matter of hours of his first spell in the trenches."*

In 1917 a German withdrawal: *"did briefly introduce a war of movement on the Western Front and provide the cavalry an opportunity to show its stuff. As mounted troops the Strathconas made their first contact with the enemy on March 26 when they cleared a wood and captured the village of Equancourt. Casualties were light: one officer (Major J.A. Critchley), and four other ranks were wounded..."* (Fraser)

Alfred wrote: *"In 1917 my brother Jack died of wounds at the age of twenty-four. He was in temporary command of Strathcona's Horse, and was hit by shrapnel in the last attack made on trenches by cavalry. Writing from hospital the day before he died, he said he was very tired but hoped to return soon. It was a great blow for my stepmother and father. Jack had twice been asked to take a staff appointment, but he liked the men, he liked his horses and he felt that perhaps too many of us were going to staff appointments. So he stayed on with the regiment."*

His death in action is reported in General Seely's book *Adventure:*

...The attack was an overwhelming success. All three regiments galloped forward to their pre-ordained positions with great speed and with surprisingly little loss.

Strathcona's captured Equancourt, and all the Germans who were not killed or captured fled in confusion.

While the officers were going back with the messages, I went round the captured positions. Major Critchley...went round with me in the fading light. He seemed curiously sad and tired, in contrast to all his men who were elated by victory. I asked him to sit down and rest whilst his officers took me round, but he insisted on coming as far as the most important point.

He explained the position to me lucidly and very slowly. And then sat down. I turned to the Sergeant-Major, who said, 'He's been shot through the chest, sir, but he made me promise not to tell until he had finished his work.'

Will it be believed that this gallant soul had been shot at close range through the lung, and still would not give in until his task was done.

We managed to get him to an Advance Dressing Station that evening, and to a Casualty Clearing Station next morning. He lingered on for two days, but then, alas, he died to the great grief of every man in Strathcona's and the Brigade."

Jack was reported as being "severely wounded in the back" on March 26 1917 and died later at No.5 Casualty Clearing Station".

W R Critchley, A C Critchley, Oswald Asheton Critchley (father), John Asheton Critchley

William Strafford Curtis

DoB: April 14 1888

Regt: London (Civil Service Rifles)

CGS: 1900-3

DoD: May 27 1915

Age: 27

Commemorated: Le Touret Memorial, France

William Strafford (or Stafford - there is some disagreement) Curtis was born in Gloucestershire from where his parents Thomas (a railway engine driver) and Elizabeth originated. He was the youngest of four children. After leaving the Grammar School, William became a school teacher.

The British attack on the Aubers Ridge began on May 9 1915. *"The Civil Service Rifles in the Great War"* by Jill Knight stated: *"The battalion's role at Festubert was alternately to hold the line and provide working parties, particularly for repairing the sandbagged breastworks which passed for trenches in the low-lying, swampy ground. They were also called upon to provide bombing parties and make almost nightly patrols in No-Man's Land. Festubert was afterwards regarded as the Civil Service Rifles's baptism of fire. Though they were not sent 'over the top', it was here that they first suffered significant casualties."* The Battle of Festubert was effectively over by May 25 and on May 27 the battalion was engaged in "cleaning the captured trench, evacuating prisoners and casualties and burying the dead...They were still under constant shell fire. Lieutenant Roberts described the appalling scene: *"Everywhere the most awful collection of debris of all sorts, dead men, dying men, equipment, clothing, rifles twisted and bent in the most fantastic shapes. Literally piles of dead men one on top of another in pools of blood. A veritable shambles and a place of utter desolation as the result of the fearful artillery fire it had undergone followed by the bombing and bayonet charges".*

Edward Stanley Curwen

DoB: January 21 1879

Regt: York and Lancaster

CGS: 1891-98

DoD: July 1 1916

Age: 37

Commemorated: Thiepval Memorial, France

Edward was the son of Canon Edward Hassell Curwen, D.C.L., and Eleanor Maria Louise Curwen (née Hill) of Kirkandrews, Carlisle. He was born at Plumbland, Cumberland where his father was the vicar. He had an older sister, Frances Edith Mackenzie Curwen. Edward had been named after his paternal grandfather, Edward Stanley Curwen, a magistrate and former Dragoon Guardsman, of Workington Hall. The ruins of Workington Hall now stand in Curwen Park. The Curwens had been Lords of the Manor for hundreds of years.

Edward was educated at Carlisle Grammar School from 1891 to 1898. He was on the school's Rugby, football and cricket teams in 1897, and won the swimming cup in 1896 and 1897. After finishing school, Edward went up to Oxford where he read English Literature. He graduated as a Bachelor of Arts in 1902 and received his Masters in 1910 (though this had demanded no further study). At Queen's, the Provost reported that Edward was: *"healthy & strong, used to play cricket & fives, can sing, interest in old books"*. Edward was a member of the Oxford University Rifle Volunteer Corps.

Edward went on to become a classics master at Rotherham Grammar School.

After the declaration of war, Edward enlisted in Sheffield in 1914, as a private, becoming a lance corporal in "A" Company, of the 12th Battalion, York and Lancaster Regiment.

He was killed on the Somme, at Serre, on July 1 1916. In the group photograph we have of him (page 134), it is poignant to note that three of the four men did not survive that first terrible day of battle on the Somme.

Arthur Edward Basil Dixon

DoB: September 26 1889

Regt: Loyal North Lancashire

CGS: 1899 - 1903

DoD: June 6 1915

Age: 25

Buried: Hop Store Cemetery, Belgium

Arthur was the son of Francis Peter and Jane Dixon. The family business had been cotton manufacturing for several generations, Dixon's chimney is still a major landmark in Carlisle. The family sold the business in 1883. Arthur's great-grandfather another Peter had established a large family home at Holme Eden In 1861. His son, yet another Peter, was there with his family and they had a dozen servants living in. Both grandsons lived there with a large extended family. The Dixon family was well known in Carlisle's political circles, Arthur's father was Mayor of Carlisle on four occasions; his great-grandfather had also been mayor, his great-great uncle had been High Sheriff of Cumberland and an M.P. Other members of the family had also held public office.

Arthur's great-grandfather was a devout Christian and he provided the land, and paid for the construction of St.Paul's Church at Holme Eden which was consecrated by the Bishop of Carlisle in 1845.

Arthur was destined for the cotton trade. After leaving Carlisle Grammar School in 1903, he attended Denstone College (1903-8) with his brother Peter and then he went to Bolton to gain experience in Messers Dobson & Barlow's cotton works. He is listed as a cotton spinning apprentice in 1911. The family must have believed that the sons should learn the business from the bottom up! He then went to a cotton mill in Lille.

With the outbreak of war Arthur joined as a private, and was promoted rapidly to 2nd Lieutenant (1914) and Lieutenant (1915). He was shot through the head on Sunday June 6 1915 and died that evening. He was buried in a plantation near where he fell. The following is part of his obituary in the Cumberland News *"Lieutenant T.O.Smith a brother officer, sends the following account of the funeral, under the date June 9th*

"I managed to get a coffin made. The man who made it was a skilled workman and made a good job of it. It was plain wood, stained oak, with a cross on the lid which was raised and ran the whole length and breadth of the coffin. Major Griffiths and I, accompanied by several of our men, attended at the graveside, when the Rev.J.C.Kennior [a friend of the late Lieutenant Dixon] conducted the burial service. Whilst we were waiting to convey the coffin to the grave the Germans started shelling all around us. They wounded one of the R.A.M.C. men but otherwise did no damage. Our own men carried the coffin to the grave, where his remains were laid to rest in a quiet and solemn manner befitting one who has given his all in his country's cause. It is very sad that an efficient soldier and a good fellow like him should die, but war demands its toll and the price must be paid in human lives".

Arthur's parents who were serving as Mayor and Mayoress in 1915, received telegrams of condolence from the King and Queen, and Lord Kitchener. In January 1916 his parents applied for permission to place a brass plaque on the wall of St. Paul, Carlisle to read

"To the beloved memory of Arthur Edward Basil Dixon, Lieutenant 5th Loyal North Lancashire Regiment, youngest son of Francis Peter Dixon, Mayor of Carlisle, born 26th September 1889; killed in action Ypres 6th June 1915 buried at Vlamertinghe Military Cemetery [sic], Belgium".

The plaque when it was finally erected in St. Cuthbert's Church, Carlisle was to Arthur and his brother Peter who was killed three years later. According to the Commonwealth War Graves Commission Arthur is buried at Hop Store Cemetery and not at Vlamertinghe. We have visited his grave at Hop Store.

Peter Sydenham Dixon

Dob: January 12 1883

Regt: Royal Sussex

CGS: 1892 -97

DoD: August 7 1918

Age: 35

Buried: Ribemont Communal Cemetery Ext, France

See Arthur Edward Dixon's entry for family background.

Peter unlike his two brothers Arthur and Francis was not destined for the family business. After leaving Carlisle Grammar School he went to Denstone College and by 1901 was articled as a solicitor's clerk, serving his articles with Mr. C.B.Hodgson, Clerk of the Peace for Cumberland. He qualified as a solicitor in 1905 and went to Hong Kong.

Whilst based in Hong Kong he visited China on an extended holiday. He kept a travel diary and his account of his five week journey to China was published in the April 1914 issue of *"The Carliol"*.

With the outbreak of war in 1914 Peter joined the Hong Kong Volunteers. By May 1916 he was a Second Lieutenant in the Royal Sussex Regt., and he was promoted to Lieutenant in 1917. In the army his legal training was used in courts martial. He was killed near Albert in France in 1918.

According to his obituary in the Cumberland News (August 17 1918) *"His letters home up to the last were always of the cheeriest description for he was possessed of a fine sense of humour, which frequently found expression in excellent short stories, some of which had been accepted for publication in "The Queen", "The Windsor Magazine" and other periodicals."*

Edward Leslie Dixon

DoB: August 23 1896

Regt: DLI

CGS: 1911-14

DoD: January 11 1916

Age: 19

Buried: Bailleul Communal Cemetery Extension Nord, France

Edward was Cumbrian through and through. He was one of three sons. His father Nicol Dixon was a grocer's manager.

Edward was good at sport; he particularly enjoyed Rugby, playing for the school and Silloth Rugby Club. On leaving school he became a chemist's apprentice.

His Army service was short. He fought in the Battle of Loos, dying of his wounds in No. 2 Casualty Clearing Station, France. A letter to the family from his commanding officer read: *"he was killed in the execution of an important and dangerous duty (he was guarding an important bridge). He was wounded by shell fire and died after removal to hospital. Your son had earned the respect and esteem of his brother soldiers...I had already secured his promotion to corporal in order to give him opportunities of learning to command. His battalion loses a good comrade and the army a promising young life".* After his death a memorial service was held which was *"packed with a sympathetic congregation"* who heard the Rev. RA Humble speak of the "admirable qualities" of Corporal Dixon.

On his grave is inscribed *"Old Carliol. Floreat Schola Carliolensis"*. Clearly his education had meant a lot to his family; so much that they would inscribe the Grammar School motto on his last resting place: *"In Carlisle will education flourish."*

John Dixon

DoB: January 20 1890

Regt: Alberta

CGS: 1905-9

DoD: April 9 1917

Age: 27

Commemorated: Vimy Memorial, France

John was the eldest of nine children born to John Dixon and his wife Mary Elizabeth Horn Mellish. His parents had married in Carlisle and they set up home with Mary's childless maternal aunt and uncle, William and Hannah Bell who farmed at Stainton, near Carlisle. John's paternal grandparents Simpson and Margaret Dixon, also had a farm at Stainton. His maternal grandparents had married at Penrith and grandfather, James Mellish, had been a coal merchant. In the 1901 census John is living with his parents, Mellish grandparents and great -uncle William Bell at Stainton. The majority of this extended family were farmers.

John attended the grammar school for four years. None of his brothers followed him; therefore it seems likely that he had won a scholarship. Whilst at school he was a keen cricketer, he won the cricket shield in 1907 and in *The Carliol* magazine he is praised several times for his bowling, but at best was only "*a fair bat or fielder*". He also played football and Rugby, but as a wing 3/4 he was apparently "*hampered by his lack of weight*", however this lack of weight enabled him to do well at the steeplechase and he came second in the egg and spoon race! John was also on the sports day committee and an active member of the debating society. In his final year he was in the pupil teacher class. According to the memorial register he became an uncertified teacher at Stanwix Council School. On July 4 1913 he sailed from Liverpool to Quebec, listing his profession as teacher.

John joined the 44th Canadian Battalion, at Winnipeg, Manitoba on May 11 1915. He is listed on the embarkation roll as a lance corporal, and he gave his father back in Carlisle as his next of kin. He had no previous military service. The 44th Battalion went to England on the SS Lapland on October 23 1915. When he died he was in the 10th Battalion, so must have transferred to that unit. The war diary for the 10th Battalion for April 8 1917 states that they were at Ecoivres and it says,

"There was no change in the disposition of companies and detachments in the line or in billets in ECOIVRES. During the early hours of the morning the parties of the Battalion carried out a raid on the enemy trenches, capturing 2 prisoners and obtaining much valuable information.
Our casualties were not heavy. 2 Officers KILLED 3 Other Ranks KILLED 13 Other Ranks wounded".

No casualties were recorded the next day, the day John died, so possibly he was one of those wounded on the 8th but didn't die until the next day.

Rugby Football - First XV - 1908 - John Dixon is on the left, front row.

38

Robert James Dixon

DoB: July 8 1893

Regt: Middlesex

CGS: 1907-12

DoD: January 23 1917

Age: 23

Buried: Madras, Chennai, India

Robert was the eldest son of Richard and Maria Dixon, 24 Portland Place, Carlisle. His father was an engine fitter.

Robert was in the Rugby team 1910-11: *"Plays a dazzling game and goes through on his own with success"* and *"A hard worker with plenty of pluck. A little more weight would make him quite a dangerous man in attack: must learn to take his passes on the run."* He won the Football Shield 1912*"Very strong tackler, is somewhat handicapped by his height, but uses what he has to great advantage, and does brilliant individual work."*

He was also a keen debater and argued against the motion that *"Cricket was a finer game than Football."* and he also argued against the motion that *"the ambitious policy of Germany is a menace to the British Empire."*

Robert joined the Territorial Force in November 1912. His attestation papers reveal he was 5'5"and had good vision and physical development. He was recommended for the 10th Battalion Middlesex Regiment and travelled to India on October 29 1914. He was made acting lance-corporal from October 1916 and is recorded as being a lance corporal when he died. He was admitted to hospital on January 15 1917 and died suddenly in Lucknow on January 28 1917 of paratyphoid or enteric fever. In a newspaper death announcement Robert is described as a *"dearly loved son"* and his death *"deeply regretted."*

Nathaniel George Dobson

DoB: May 30 1892

Regt: Cameronians

CGS: 1904 - 8

DoD: November 17 1918

Age: 26

Buried: St. Sever Cemetery, Rouen, France

Thanks to the Dobson family

Nathaniel was born and brought up at Harrington near Workington. His father had begun his career as a commercial traveller and then settled in Harrington as a grocer. Nathaniel's brother Charles followed their father into the family business. His grandfather Dobson had been a sea captain and his maternal grandfather was a miller. He attended the Grammar School for three years and played in the school cricket team. After leaving school he trained to become an electrical engineer and worked for the Newcastle Power Station Company.

Nathaniel had an extremely confused war service. On enlistment (Dec 1915) he joined the Artists Rifles, went into the reserves and wasn't mobilised until February 5 1917. His great-niece says that he had wanted to go into the Royal Engineers as he was an electrical engineer however he was put in the Royal Flying Corps as a 2nd Lieutenant. However things did not go well in the RFC, and within four months he was given a medical discharge as being permanently unfit to be a pilot or observer due to nervous instability.

He was recommended to be sent to the Royal Engineers but instead ended up in the Border Regt, attached to the 1st Cameronians. He was transferred back to the infantry on November 3 1917.

Nathaniel arrived in Boulogne on October 15 1918, and joined his unit on October 21. The next day the battalion moved forward to positions near the Selle River. In the early hours of the following day, the battalion attacked reaching the northern edge of Vendecies Wood, where they took up positions. The following night, October 24/25 the positions were heavily shelled, with gas and artillery shells. On October 25 the battalion captured Ence Fontaine. Nathaniel, according to the battalion war diary was wounded on Oct 25, and other sources say two days earlier. He had gunshot wounds to his left leg, and both arms. His right arm had to be amputated at the elbow. He had shrapnel wounds to his face too. He was moved from the casualty clearing station to the hospital in Rouen and died there three weeks later at 8.15am on November 17 1918. His family had been given permission to travel to visit him in hospital; unfortunately he died before they reached him. The armistice had been signed just a week earlier.

Nathaniel's RFC ID bracelet recently came up for sale and is now owned by a collector in New Zealand. Nathaniel left an estate worth £242 10s 2d. His mother applied for his medals in 1920.

Trinity School pupils and staff looking for the graves of past pupils of Carlisle Grammar School. Staff on the trip were: the two authors, Jessie Southwell, Tom Snaith and Marcel McLean.

Joseph Dodd

DoB: February 7 1892

Regt: CEF

CGS: 1906-8

DoD: September 26 1916

Age: 24

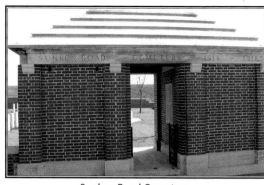
Sunken Road Cemetery.

Buried: Sunken Road Cemetery, near Albert, France.

Joseph was the youngest of ten children born to Rosanna (née Potts) and William Dodd. The Dodd family of Greystead, Northumberland were numerous and William was well known as an enthusiastic fox hunter and he had the nickname *'Long Sally'*, as he was 6ft 7" tall!

Whilst at school Joseph was awarded prizes for maths, and for running the mile and the three mile cross-country steeplechase on sports day. According to the school register he became a journalist. However on enlistment he described himself as a farmer. On the 1911 census he was in London and said he was a student in the Civil Service. A Joseph Dodd *'journalist'* arrived in Canada in 1914. He may have gone to join one of his older brothers who lived there.

Joseph joined up within days of war being declared. He enlisted at Winnipeg, Manitoba on October 27 1914. He was described as 5ft 10 ½ ", with a fair complexion and blue eyes. He joined the 27th (City of Winnipeg) Battalion of the Canadian Expeditionary Force. His battalion was not sent to Europe for another year arriving in September 1915 as part of the Canadian Corps. They did not participate in any major offensive until the following year. The battle at St.Eloi (April 1916) was a baptism of fire for them; the next major encounter with the enemy was on the Somme. They moved there in September. By the end of October 20,000 Canadians lay dead including Joseph who died September 26 1916 during the battle for Thiepval Ridge.

Edward Hughes Dodgson

DoB: September 5 1876

Regt: Royal Engineers

CGS: 1893 - 5

DoD: May 3 1918

Age: 41

Aire Communal Cemetery.

Buried: Aire Communal Cemetery, France

Edward Hughes Dodgson was the youngest son of Cockermouth doctor Henry Dodgson and his wife Frances. Edward along with his older brother was first sent to Pocklington Grammar School in Yorkshire and then moved to Carlisle Grammar School. Edward made an impact on the sports field; he was good at the steeplechase and the "The Carliol" published the following glowing tribute to him in July 1895 "We are sorry to say that our athletics will suffer by the retirement from our midst of……….and E.H.Dodgson. We can only say that we hope they will do as well in their new careers as they have in the cricket field"

Edward became a land agent and surveyor and married Annie Ritson in the summer of 1913. His war record is a little confusing he was in the 5th Battalion the Border Regiment when it was mobilised on August 4 1914. There is a mention of him being a Lieutenant in 1914. The CGS register says he was a Captain in the Border Regiment.

The Cumberland News reported that Captain Dodgson was: "a good officer to the men, very level-headed, will be stern with the men where it is needed, and I must say all through is very human."

The CWGC says he was a sapper in the 5th Field Survey Company of the Royal Engineers when he died in 1918. This company had been formed in 1916 and probably drew suitably qualified men from other regiments which would explain Edward's move, but not the drop in rank. He died of his wounds at a casualty clearing station. He left £2,200 in his will equivalent to £100,000 today. Of Edward's six surviving siblings none appear to have had children.

43

Charles Bertram Dove

DoB: July 6 1884

Regt: Border

CGS: 1907-12

DoD: March 21 1918

Age: 33

Buried: Favreuil Military Cemetery, France

Charles Bertram was the eldest child of John Charles Dove and Jane Anderson Wood.

Charles received a commission to the 3rd Battalion Border Regiment but he later resigned from the army and went to work at Crewe in the engineering works of the London and North Western Railway. Charles left there in 1907 after two years eight months' service. He was described as being of *"Good"* character with *"Fair"* abilities. In 1906 he went to Canada where he married Amy Caton Thompson on October 23 1914. The couple had a daughter.

On the declaration of war Charles returned to Britain and re-joined his old regiment with his former rank of Lieutenant. He went to France on Christmas Eve 1914 where he was attached to the Cornwalls and then the Devons and was then made a captain in the Border Regiment. Charles arrived to join the 2nd Battalion in May 1915, as part of a group replacing losses following the Battle of Festubert.

In 1916 he was transferred to the 11th Battalion following losses on the Somme. At some point he was attached to the 8th Battalion. He was killed while marching up on March 21 1918 as *"huge artillery fire opened...and the German heavy guns bombarded the railheads, supply depots, dumps and camps in rear... "* (Wylly). 21 March 1918 was the opening of the German Spring Offensive.

Henry Frederick Edgecumbe Edwardes

DoB: December 21 1878

Regt: Duke of Cornwall's Light Infantry

CGS: Teacher

DoD: February 6 1917

Age: 38

Bethune Town Cemetery.

Buried: Bethune Town Cemetery, France

Henry was one of five children born to Edgecumbe Ferguson Edwardes and his wife Emily Yair (née Dobson). His father was a solicitor born in India where his father was Physician General for H.M. Bombay Army.

Henry attended Crediton Grammar School, and followed in his father's footsteps by attending Cambridge University, although he went to St. John's College whereas his father had been at Trinity College. He gained his B.A. in 1900. He then became a languages teacher, firstly at Carlisle Grammar School, then at Coatham School, a school in Paris, Shrewsbury School, Kimberley Boys High School, South Africa, Wakefield Grammar School and University College School, London.

Henry enlisted on October 6 1914 in the Royal Fusiliers. He went to France on November 14 1915 as part of the BEF and was there for four months before returning to England to attend Cadet School. He was given his commission as a Second Lieutenant in the Duke of Cornwall's Light Infantry on July 6 1916. On enlistment he was described as 5ft 11" tall, weighing 154lb, with brown hair and blue eyes. He died in a raid on enemy trenches eight months after receiving his commission. The raid took twenty minutes and only two men died.

Herbert Ronald Farrar

DoB: July 25 1887

Regt: Leicester

CGS: 1897-8

DoD: December 24 1914

Age: 27

Buried: Dranoutre Military Cemetery, Belgium

Dulwich College

Ronald was born at South Shields, County Durham, the second child of the Rev. Herbert W. Farrar's second marriage, to Florence Margaret Town. Ronald was not a pupil at Carlisle Grammar School for very long. After moving to Dulwich School, he studied the classics and went up to his father's college of Queens' in Cambridge in 1906. While there he served as a Sergeant in the University Officers' Training Corps (O.T.C.), and graduated with a B.A. in 1910. *"From 1910 to 1912 he worked as an assistant master at Ripplevale Preparatory School in Kent, before joining the staff at Windlesham House (Gentlemen's) School, at Norfolk Terrace, Brighton for Michaelmas term 1912. In the RagDance on the last Saturday of his first term, he dressed as an Arab sheikh. He also opened the batting for the staff XI in summer 1913, scoring one run. In the spring of 1914 he travelled in the South of France, sailed up the Nile in Egypt as far as Aswan and came home via the Italian Lakes."*

On the day war was declared, August 4 1914, Ronald volunteered for service in the Public Schools Battalion. Although he was said not to be physically strong, his experience in the O.T.C. at Cambridge led to a probationary commission as a 2nd lieutenant in the 3rd (Reserve) Battalion of the Leicestershire Regiment. He left for France on October 27 and was attached to the 2nd Battalion Manchester Regiment, in charge of two platoons and shot two of the enemy. By December 1 1914 the battalion had reached Dranoutre, near Ypres, Belgium and were resting in their billets. During the next week they received an 'appreciative address' from their commanding officer, took in reinforcements and, according to the battalion's war diary records, played football...As the month progressed, they moved from trench to trench under regular shellfire. *'The division was now holding a line from La Petite Douve in a northwest direction up the slope to the Wulverghem-Mesines road and to the east to Hill 75,covering a front of about 3,500 yards. The weather was wet and cold, and the trenches were knee-deep in mud and water'.*

They received a break from the action during the week before Christmas when they *"rested in billets"* and attended a church parade on December 20.

Returning to the Front, the battalion moved to trenches east of Lindenhoek on December 23 and on Christmas Eve took over old trenches at Wulvergham from the Bedford Regiment. The weather changed to a hard frost, making trench conditions a little more bearable than the sticky mud they were used to. The sound of carols and hymns could be heard from the trenches on both sides, and the heavy guns stopped firing during the unofficial 'Christmas Truce'. German troops coming into the lines brought Christmas trees to place on their parapets, but vigilance was still necessary. Records show that even on this day of low fatalities, 98 British soldiers died, many the victims of sniper fire. The battalion war diary records that amongst the unlucky few to die that day were 2nd Lt.H.R.Farrar and a Sergeant Williams. Ronald was buried on Christmas Day 1914, in Dranoutre churchyard, attended by the general and many officers of the regiment.

A letter from Helen Moses, of the VAD Hospital in Beckenham, Kent, asking for Ronald's parents' address is in the Archives at Kew. She wrote on behalf of a soldier to whom Farrar had been kind. He wanted to express his gratitude.

(Much of this account comes from the research by Ian Hilder, and the rest from the History of the Manchester Regiment)

Charles Cecil Forster

DoB: August 10 1888

Regt: Leicestershire

CGS: 1904-07

DoD: September 26 1917

Age: 29

Commemorated: Tyne Cot Memorial, Belgium

Thanks to the Forster family

Charles was born at Great Orton, Cumbria, where his father was teaching. He was the fourth child of eight children of James Forster and Elizabeth Ann Harrison.

Charles was one of the first students to attend Sunderland Teacher Training College. It was established in 1908 for day students only. In the 1911 census Charles was resident at 41 Broad St. Carlisle working as an assistant teacher. His younger siblings Florence, Ethel, and Harold were also living with him.

During the Great War Charles was in the 2/4th Battalion Leicestershire Regiment and was awarded Victory and British medals (he probably did not serve in 1914/15) The Battalion was in Ireland in 1916 for the Easter Uprising and returned to England in January 1917 when Charles married Eliza(Leila) Marshall (1887-1962). She was born in Dovenby to parents William and Fanny Marshall - William was Head of Dovenby School. The Battalion returned to France on February 24 1917. Charles was almost certainly killed on the first day of the Battle of Polygon Wood. His service record has not been found. He is also commemorated on the memorial at Calthwaite church. His death is recorded in the school log by his father who added, on the day the news was received: *"no singing in Assembly today as headmaster not in a singing mood".* Eliza never remarried. After the death of her new husband she continued to work in an art shop in Carlisle. She is buried in Carlisle cemetery with her mother and sister, with whom she lived after Charles' death at Greystoke Road, Carlisle.

Robert Clow Foster

DoB: May 19 1892

Regt: Suffolk

CGS: 1904-07

DoD: April 10 1918

Age: 25

Commemorated: Ploegsteert Memorial, Belgium

Courtesy of Kings College , University of London

Robert was born in Carlisle and was of Scottish descent. Robert lived with his uncle and aunt, John and Frances Foster. His uncle was head teacher of St John's Boys School in Carlisle. The couple seem to have "adopted" a clever boy as their nephew attended Carlisle Grammar School and then went to King's College, London University where he achieved his degree.

Robert was originally a private in the London Regiment, and then in June 1917 he was commissioned into the Suffolk Regiment as an officer. The 11th Battalion Suffolk Regiment Resources website reports: *"Thus the first troops of the 34th Division to enter the general engagement were those who, almost up to that very moment, had formed the corps reserve, a rare tactical anomaly. Terrific fighting followed. On the 10th April the 11th Suffolks, having formed a defensive flank, beat off attack after attack. Twice the Germans broke through, but on one occasion the breach was closed by Captain Rodwell and his company, assisted by Major Wright. At 3:20 p.m. Lieut.-Colonel Tuck received orders to withdraw behind the Lys. Speaking on the telephone, the officer commanding the battalion next on the left, which was still in the front line, explained that he could not possibly get clear in less than two hours. Colonel Tuck replied that in these circumstances he would do his best to hold on until five o'clock. He did so; and though the casualties in those two hours were heavy, this noble imposition helped materially to save two brigades."* Robert was recorded as having been killed in action.

James Whaley Fryer

DoB: February 25 1892

Regt: Northumberland Fusiliers

CGS: 1905-10

DoD: July 1 1916

Age: 24

Commemorated: Thiepval Memorial, France

James was the son of Major James Whaley Fryer and Edith Hindhaugh. He had a sister, Dorothy Elizabeth Fryer. The family lived at Hawes, Yorkshire. James was educated at Yorebridge Grammar School, Hawes, Giggleswick School and Carlisle Grammar School.

He became an articled clerk to Messrs. Dickinson, Millar & Turnbull, solicitors, Newcastle-upon-Tyne and was just about to qualify when he joined the Northumberland Fusiliers (22nd Battalion Tyneside Scottish), shortly after the outbreak of war. He went to France on January 10 1916 and was killed by a shell as he climbed over the trench parapet attacking La Boiselle on the first day of the Battle of the Somme. The Craven Herald of 1 September 1916 reported:

"Second-Lieutenant J. Whaley Fryer, Northumberland Fusiliers, only son of the late Major Fryer, Rookhurst, Hawes, and Mrs. Fryer, Moorside, Fenham, Newcastle, who was reported missing in the big push in July, is now reported killed. Mrs. Fryer has received the following letter from the captain commanding the company:-

"Whaley was in my Company, and I have been informed by some of the men in the Company that they saw him fall. It is very sad, but I am afraid he was killed; he fell just after he got over the top of the parapet. He was very well liked by all the men and also got on well with all the officers in the Battalion."

Richard Parker Gilbanks

DoB: April 4 1892

Regt: Border

CGS: 1905-8

DoD: August 9 1915

Age: 23

Commemorated: Helles Memorial, Turkey

Richard Parker Gilbanks was born at the Rectory in the pretty village of Gt. Orton just a few miles outside Carlisle. He was one of a large family, with an equally large extended family. His father William Foster Gilbanks and grandfather George were both ordained ministers and at least one uncle was ordained too. Richard was also studying for the ministry when war broke out. His grandfather had been Vicar of Smethwick, Staffordshire for many years. However, his roots were Cumbrian. On his mother's side his grandfather William Parker was a Justice of the Peace and lived at Carleton Hill, Penrith, for many years, he left over £35,000 when he died in 1892.

Richard attended Mr Allen's Prep School at Silloth, and then came to the grammar school as a day pupil. Whilst at the grammar school he won the Latin Prize (1908). He went on to Rossall School and then Trinity College, Oxford. He matriculated on October 13 1911 and was awarded a fourth class honours in modern history in 1914. The degree of BA was conferred on February 13 1915. Trinity College was able to provide his photograph, as he was a member of *"The Claret Club"*, which was and still is a dining club. Of the nine members in the photograph four of them lost their lives in the war. Richard had many friends and his obituary gives further details of his full and active social life.

He went straight from Oxford to the army and he joined the 6th Border Regt as soon as war broke out and became a second lieutenant on August 25 1914. He is described as 5ft 10 3/8" tall and weighing 144lb. He was sent out to the Dardanelles as part of the Mediterranean Expeditionary Force in July 1915. In August 1915, he was part of 'B' Company attacking Chocolate Hill at Gallipoli. The attack began on August 6. On August 9 the orders were to attack the Turkish position; by 9.30 in the morning all the officers, including Richard, were dead.

In his army personal file his place of death is listed as Suvla Bay, Dardanelles. His burial place is unknown.

Richard is also commemorated on the village war memorial in the churchyard at Great Orton. One of the other eight names is that of a local farmer's son George Norman, who also attended the grammar school.

Gilbanks, back right, the Claret Club, 1914, Oxford.

Robert de Glanville

DoB: October 18 1896 (probable)

Regt: Cameron Highlanders

CGS: 1912–13

DoD: September 26 1915

Age: 18

Commemorated: Loos Memorial

Courtesy Ashby Museum

Robert was born in Burma, to Sir Oscar de Glanville, an Irish barrister who became President of the Burmese Legislative Council and married a Burmese woman. They had three children.

Robert had attended Ashby de la Zouch grammar school in Leicestershire where Charles Frederick Christian Padel was headmaster. In 1912 Mr Padel moved to take up the post of headmaster in Carlisle. Douglas Hannay and Robert de Glanville were two of at least five pupils who made the move to Carlisle from Ashby de la Zouch between 1912-3. Robert was a real asset to the school as he was an excellent cricketer and he was in the Rugby team too. He was a house prefect and a keen member of the debating society. He opposed two motions one of which probably reflects his experience *"that constant travelling narrows a man's intellect"*, he also opposed the motion *"that modern warfare does not pay the victor"*. His all round sports ability meant that he was awarded the "Senior Challenge Cup" in 1913.

After leaving Carlisle Grammar School Robert went to Glasgow University to study engineering. However he was there for only a short time as he signed up for active service on September 8 1914. Like many hundreds of other recruits Robert lied when he signed up and added two years to his age, saying he was 19 years and 11 months when he was probably only 17 years and 11 months.

He joined the 6th Battalion Queen's Own Cameron Highlanders. He was 5 feet 6 ½ inches tall and 133lbs, with a dark complexion, dark hair and brown eyes.

Robert died at Loos. Unusually there is an account of his death written by a Private David D Munro, who lay beside him on the battlefield for the last hour of his life; he said that he died peacefully. The following day there was no trace of his body as there had been further shelling. He had been in France just 79 days. It is nice to note that Private Munro survived the war and was demobbed in 1919.

"*The Carliol*" Magazine at first listed Robert as wounded, then as a POW, before his death was finally confirmed.

The following was in The Carliol magazine in the spring edition of 1917. *From Private Norman Shaw, 3rd Cameron Highlanders*

"*Since I returned to this depot I have come into contact with numerous members of De Glanville's old battalion...All speak well of him, and from what I hear his courage and pluck were splendid. These characteristics endeared him to his comrades, but not so much as another virtue of his – his unselfishness. Lance-Corporal Spence told me of how De Glanville often gave up his rations to any young boy in the trenches. That, I think, is a more meritorious deed than going out to help a wounded man. Again, I have heard of his perpetual desire to be doing something useful, and, as a result he was greatly in demand for listening posts, wiring parties and other tasks for which only volunteers are of use.*"

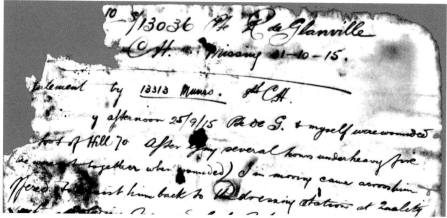

Private Munro's letter re- De Glanville - Displayed in full on page 133.

James Graham

DoB: January 1 1887

Regt: Gloucester

CGS: 1903-5

DoD: October 24 1918

Age: 31

Buried: Pommereuil, France

Pommereuil Cemetery.

James was the eldest of three children born to John William Graham and his wife Mary Teresa (née McCauley). James was to become the fourth generation of the Grahams to be involved in the cab business which had been founded by his great-grandfather. He married Aida Agnes Kellet in 1913; they had a house on Petteril Street.

James first served in the Royal Army Service Corps (R.A.S.C.) His deployment to this branch of the army makes perfect sense given his experience with the family cab firm. The R.A.S.C. was responsible for land, coastal and lake transport; air despatch; of all non ordnance supplies for the army e.g. food, water, fuel, and clothing. James was transferred to the Gloucester Regiment. In November 1917 the regiment went to Italy and returned to France in September 1918 It was attached to the 75th Brigade in the 25th Division. It seems likely that James died in the Battle of the Selle.

On October 24, the Battalion War Diary recorded:-

Fine. C9.15. the Battalion was relieved by the KING'S OWN SHROPSHIRE LIGHT INFANTRY & withdrew to & concentrated at PLAQUET BRIFAUT, moving back to POMMEREUIL at 20.00 hrs. arriving into cellars at 21.00 hrs.

James Graham was one of six fatalities from the battalion that day, and they were probably killed during the relief. He is buried at Pommereuil.

William Graham

DoB: August 19 1894

Regt: Border

CGS: 1908 - 13

DoD: July 1 1916

Age: 21

Commemorated: Thiepval Memorial, France

William was the eleventh child of 13 born to William Graham and Mary (née Gilbertson). William senior is listed as a labourer and a gamekeeper, so it seems likely that William junior was a scholarship pupil. The family lived in the Kingstown/Stanwix area from 1882 onwards. William and Mary had been married at Longtown in 1877 and their first two children were born there. Mary was born in Dumfries-shire and her family moved to Longtown when she was very young. Her mother died in 1881 which may explain the move to Stanwix. Her widowed father and siblings also moved to the Stanwix area. Both of William's grandfathers had been agricultural labourers like his father.

William attended the Grammar School as a pupil from 1908-11 and then as a pupil teacher from 1911-13. He then became a schoolmaster.

William enlisted in Carlisle in the 11th Battalion the Border Regt., better known as the Lonsdales. The Lonsdales had been formed by the Earl of Lonsdale and it was a "pals battalion". William was in B company which was made up of men from North and West Cumbria and landed in France on the November 23 1915.

He was a corporal but at the time of his death he was acting sergeant. On July 1 1916 the battalion were at AUTHUILLE WOOD, the War Diary states

"Zero time 7.30 am. Battalion advanced from assembly trenches at 8 am and came under very heavy machine gun fire suffering over 500 casualties."

56

Colonel H.C. Wylly, C.B., author of 'The Border Regiment in the Great War' writes:

"(on 1st July) the objective was Mouquet Farm...the Lonsdale Battalion had to move N. out of Authuille Wood for some little distance and then swing due E.;this movement... had not only to be calculated exactly as to time, but had to be done under heavy fire...On leaving their trenches in the wood, even before arriving at the front British trench, the Battalion came under a terrific machine gun fire..There was no question of flinching; the companies, men dropping every moment, moved steadily on...The attacking line, supported by the Lonsdales, was having a hard fight to try and reach the German trenches, but few were able to get so far since the enemy machine guns were taking a terrible toll, mowing down the men in scores and causing very heavy losses.

...within a very short time out of the 28 officers and 800 other ranks who left the wood, 25 officers and some 500 non-commissioned officers and men were out of action. Men could do no more."

Wylly pg 84

William was unaccounted for when a roll call was taken the next day. And his death was assumed November 18 1916.

This school cricket team photograph features five of the subjects of this book namely:
R De Glanville, W Graham (front right), H L Simpson, W Sinclair, T H Mellish.

Douglas Ronald Maurice Hannay

DoB: April 16 1897

Regt: Royal Marine Light Infantry

CGS: 1912-4

DoD: November 7 1917

Age: 20

Tyne Cot Cemetery.

Commemorated: Tyne Cot, Belgium

Douglas was the youngest of nine children born to John and Mary Hannay of Pouton, Garlieston, Wigtownshire. The Hannay family were long established in the area. His father had a large farm of 320 acres and was an accountant too. Douglas however, was born in Glasgow, at his maternal grandparents' home. His maternal grandfather, William Cairney was a shipbroker. The family employed servants and had a governess for Douglas's sisters.

Douglas came to Carlisle grammar school from Ashby de la Zouch grammar school in 1912. Robert de Glanville had also made the move from Ashby the previous term. They were both boarders.

Douglas joined The Royal Marine Light Infantry on February 15 1916. He embarked with the Royal Marine Brigade on the July 12 1916, and was drafted to the British Expeditionary Force on December 18 1916, just one month after qualifying as a saddler. He was at Calais base Depot on December 19 and in January 1917 was attached to the 8th Entrenching Battalion. In February 1917 he joined the 2nd Royal Marine Battalion, and was briefly drafted as an orderly to the 188th Infantry Brigade before returning to the 2nd Royal Marine Battalion, he died on Passchendaele Ridge on November 7 1917, and was reported missing in the 1918 edition of *"The Carliol"* magazine.

James Blackwood Hay

DoB: October 18 1887

Regt: York and Lancaster

CGS: 1900-6

DoD: October 29 1918

Houghton Hall

Age: 31

Buried: Staglieno Cemetery, Genoa, Italy

James was the only son of James and Jane Hay. His father was head gardener at Houghton Hall, Houghton. Both his parents came from Scotland.

James first attended Houghton Voluntary School then went to the Grammar School in 1900, and became a George Moore Exhibitioner in 1902. He was head of school in his final year, 1906. He then went to Armstrong College, Newcastle-upon-Tyne, which is now part of Newcastle University. He graduated in 1909 with a B.Litt. He was awarded a masters degree in 1916. After leaving Armstrong College he taught at four secondary schools, in Montrose, Wem, Sheffield and finally at Ashbourne, Derbyshire.

James enlisted in Carlisle in June 1916, and was called up four months later. He was a private in the Liverpool Regiment. He applied for a commission within weeks of enlistment. He served in France for two weeks in February 1917, and was then recalled to England to attend cadet school. On receiving his commission in August 1917 he was promoted to second lieutenant and he joined the York and Lancaster Regiment, he went to Italy in Dec 1917. He died of influenza and broncho-pneumonia in hospital on October 29 1918. He is buried at Staglieno Cemetery, Genoa.

James married Catherine Sutton at Jesmond Wesleyan Church, Newcastle-upon-Tyne in early 1917. When he died he left an estate of £247.

Walter Henderson

Dob: November 30, 1878

Regt: Highland Light Infantry

CGS: 1893-4

Dod: March 8 1918

Age: 39

Buried: Hooge Crater Cemetery, Belgium

Walter was the third of six children born to Thomas Henderson and Martha Hind. Thomas was a beerhouse keeper in Caldewgate, Carlisle. Walter later gave his father's occupation as Hotel Proprietor (deceased). Younger brother Robert Stubbs Henderson, a Sorting Clerk and Telegraphist , died on 27 January 1917, of dysentery, a Pioneer of the Corps of Royal Engineers and was buried at Dar-es-Salaam War Cemetery.

Walter was a Scholarship boy. After attending the Grammar School, he became a teacher, training at the Fawcett School and Bede College having passed the matriculation exam of Durham University. When war was declared, Walter was a schoolmaster assistant with the City Education Committee. For several years he was secretary of Carlisle Schools Football League. He also enjoyed athletics.

Walter joined the Army soon after the outbreak of war as a private but later obtained a commission. He arrived in France with the 9th Highland Light Infantry on November 28 1917, and was killed in action on March 8 1918 on the Menin Road while attached to the Royal Fusiliers. The Cumberland News reported on the *"gallant"* way he met his death. The Major of his Battalion wrote: *"He was killed instantly by a trench mortar shell. I cannot speak too highly of the magnificent way he behaved during the very heavy bombardment by the enemy. He was out in the trench with his men the whole time cheering them up and attending to the wounded. By his death the Battalion has lost a very brave and efficient officer. He was very popular with all ranks, and his loss is keenly felt."*

Arthur Hetherington

DoB: August 20 1888

Regt: King's Own Yorkshire Light Infantry

CGS: 1905-7

DoD: March 21 1918

Pozieres Memorial France

Age: 29

Commemorated: Pozieres Memorial, France

Arthur was the youngest of ten children born to Samuel Hetherington and his wife Annie Barnfather. Both families were large and had been in the Brampton area for many generations. Samuel began his working life as a weaver but progressed to being a boot and shoe dealer. When he died in 1905 the family were living in Shields House, Brampton which had 11 rooms. Arthur joined the pupil teacher's class at the Grammar School in 1905 and stayed for two years. He attended Dundee Teacher Training College from 1911-13. He then moved to the north-east, and took a job as assistant master at Haverton Hill School near Middlesbrough.

Arthur enlisted in the Yorkshire Regiment in December 1915, he was mobilised in February 1916, and he landed in France on June 15 1916. After being awarded his commission and becoming a 2nd lieutenant he joined the 9th battalion of the King's Own Yorkshire Light Infantry. He was killed in action on March 22 1918 on the Somme during the German spring offensive.

Brampton does not have a traditional war memorial; it has a War Memorial Hospital. Inside the front door there is a huge board which dominates the reception area. It lists the men of the Brampton area who perished 1914-18. As well as Arthur, two of his cousins, Isaac and Cyril Dudley Hetherington are also listed. Arthur left £200 18s. He was engaged to be married when he died.

Harry Scott Higginson

DoB: June 28 1886

Regt: CEF

CGS: 1897-1905

DoD: August 9 1915

Age: 29

Buried: St Marie Cemetery, Le Havre, France

Harry was the eldest son of Henry Higginson, an architect born in Preston, and Wilhelmina (née Scott) from Dumfries, the daughter of a bookseller.

Harry had been a good all-round sportsman at school and was an especially good golfer. After leaving school, he trained as a land agent. In April 1914 Harry travelled to Halifax, Nova Scotia to join his brother Frank.

Harry joined up almost as soon as war had been declared. His attestation paper reveals he was 5'8" with fair hair and grey eyes. He travelled with the CEF to Salisbury Plain for training and sailed for France in February 1915. In July he was wounded in action by a bullet in the groin. After transferring to hospital, he displayed no serious symptoms for a week, but then septic poisoning set in and his condition became critical. Harry's father, having received a telegram apprising him of his son's condition, decided to go to Le Havre to see him. The permit to cross the Channel was issued too late however, and he arrived seven hours after his son had died. Frank, who had also joined up, had received a permit to leave the firing line in order to see his brother, but he also reached Le Havre too late, the train in which he travelled being held up 24 hours on the way, through an accident to another train.

Harry's funeral took place at Le Havre and was attended by his father and brother.

Beresford Karr Horan

DoB: January 14 1892

Regt: CEF

CGS: 1899

DoD: December 24 1915

Age: 23

Buried: Mount Pleasant Cemetery, London, Ontario, Canada

Beresford Karr Horan was the elder son of the Rev. Charles Trevor Horan and his wife Edith. Both families had an army and church tradition, which included service overseas, Beresford's father was born in India and was Chaplain of All Saint's Cairo when Beresford died. The Horan family also had a tradition of attending Cambridge University. Beresford's family moved around with his father's career. Beresford was born in Cambridge; he had one brother and one sister, and by the age of nine was already away at boarding school in Norfolk.

He attended the Grammar School for just one term before moving on, firstly to The Royal Naval College, Osborne, Isle of Wight, where his uncle the Rev. Frederick Seymour Horan was chaplain, and secondly to Marlborough College (1905-07). However in 1909 aged just seventeen, he defied family tradition and emigrated to Canada to farm, and was still in Ontario in 1911. Beresford is unusual amongst those on the Grammar School memorial as he died before reaching Europe so he never entered the field of battle.

He enlisted in the United States Marine Corps June 14 1913, where he served for nearly two years; he was in the band, based mainly in California. In February 1915 he is listed as a deserter from the 4th Regiment the U.S. Marines. We have been unable to find out why he deserted. However we do know that some soldiers deserted the American Army to join up elsewhere as they wished to fight and the USA did not enter the war until 1917.

Within six months Beresford had joined the 30th Wellington Rifles as part of the Canadian Expeditionary Force; he was given the rank of 2nd Lieutenant. On enlistment he was 6ft 1/2" tall, with blue eyes and brown hair. He described himself as a bank clerk and was honest about having been in the U.S. Marine Corps.

He was listed as a deserter on November 17 1915, and died on Christmas Eve 1915. The Carlisle Memorial Register and his obituary in the Cumberland News both state that he *"died from pneumonia following diphtheria contracted while training with the CEF"*. However he was in disgrace. The Canadian Army refused him a war grave as he was a deserter. But he did have a magnificent gravestone where he was laid to rest in Mount Pleasant Cemetery, London, Ontario.

Mount Pleasant Cemetery

64

Hugh Richard Hyndman -Jones

DoB: December 3 1890

Regt: AIF

CGS: 1901-03

DoD: October 4 1917

Age: 26

Commemorated: Menin Gate, Belgium

Hugh's father Richard William is recorded on the 1891 Census as having been born in Georgetown, British Guiana and his mother Alice Sophia in New South Wales, so it is perhaps unsurprising that the family should emigrate to Australia in 1903. Hugh was born in St Pancras, London, and by 1901 was at Kendal and then Carlisle Grammar School.

Hugh joined up in March 1915 in Melbourne aged 24. He was 5'7'' with blue eyes and dark brown hair and was a motor mechanic. He was sent to Gallipoli in August 1915 and disembarked at Alexandria in January 1916. From there he transferred to join the BEF in France. During that year Hugh was promoted to corporal, then sergeant. By October he had several problems with myositis (muscle inflammation), and in 1917 suffered from scabies and dermatitis, and had several admissions to hospital. Given the conditions in the trenches this is perhaps hardly unusual. In December 1916 while at Wareham in England (following a hospital admission) Hugh went AWOL for 24 hours and was *"Admonished"* and had to forfeit two days (pay? leave?).

Hugh was killed near Ypres during the Battle of Passchendaele and is remembered on the Menin Gate as HR Jones. He and his wife Dorothy had an infant son, Hugh William, living in Abbotsford, Victoria. By his will he left his wife two sets of draughtsman's Instruments, two books, curios, three pipes, cards and studs.

William Glaister Irving

DoB: April 6 1897

Navy: Mercantile Marine.

CGS: 1909-12

DoD: August 25 1917

Tower Hill Memorial, London

Age: 20

Commemorated: Tower Hill Memorial, London

William Glaister Irving was the only son of William Irving and Elizabeth (née Glaister). He was born and brought up on Eden Street, Silloth. The Irving family roots were in Dumfriesshire. William senior had a grocery shop. Most of the family had maritime trades.

William was the only member of his family to attend the Grammar School. He was a day student and a keen Rugby player. After leaving he was apprenticed to Messers. Charles E Dunn & Co., steamship owners, Liverpool. He travelled to the USA on *SS Cymrie* in 1915 describing himself as an apprentice.

William received his second mate's ticket on May 14 1917, and sailed as third mate on the *SS Sycamore* a 6,550 ton steamship, built on the Clyde and launched in 1917. William was part of a multinational crew. On August 25 1917 *SS Sycamore* was carrying general cargo from Baltimore to Liverpool when she was torpedoed without warning, sinking 125 miles north-west of the north coast of Ireland with the loss of 11 crew members, who are commemorated on memorials in the Caribbean, Newfoundland and Cheltenham.

The U-boat which sank them, UB-61, commanded by T Schultz, was sunk by a mine in the North Sea just a few weeks later on November 29 1917.

Walter Jackson

DoB: November 12 1894

Navy: Royal

CGS: 1906-08

DoD: May 31 1916_

Age: 21

HMS Warrior

Commemorated: Plymouth Memorial

Walter was the eldest son of Joseph and Rachel Jackson. He was born and brought up at Longtown.
Walter joined the Royal Navy as a first-class stoker, and was killed during the largest sea battle of the Great War - the Battle of Jutland - on May 31 1916.

He served in *HMS Warrior* which joined the Grand Fleet in December 1914. At the Battle of Jutland on May 31 1916, the 1st Cruiser Squadron flagship, *HMS Defence*, and *HMS Warrior* spotted the German II Scouting Group and opened fire, but their shells fell short. Shortly afterwards they moved in on the damaged German light cruiser *SMS Wiesbaden* but they were themselves intercepted by the German battle cruiser *SMS Derfflinger* and four other battleships. The fire from the German ships was heavy and both *HMS Defence and HMS Warrior* were hit. *HMS Warrior* was saved when the German ships switched their fire to the battleship *HMS Warspite*.

Warrior had been badly damaged by the German shells; she was flooding and suffered from large fires, although her engines continued running long enough to allow her to withdraw. She was taken in tow by *HMS Engadine* who rescued the surviving crew of 743. On June 1, she was abandoned and subsequently foundered. Walter was one of 68 men from *HMS Warrior* killed, of whom 38, including Walter, were stokers. He was buried at sea.

John Morrison Jessamine

DoB: September 28 1890

Regt: Royal Scots

CGS: 1900-7

DoD: July 1 1916

Age: 25

Thiepval Memorial, the Somme

Commemorated: Thiepval Memorial, France

John Morrison Jessamine was born on his maternal grandfather, Thomas Waugh's farm at Burgh by Sands a few miles west of Carlisle. Both he and his only sibling Thomas Waugh Jessamine attended the Grammar School. His parents, John Alexander and Jane Isabella, and three of his grandparents were born in Scotland, which may have influenced his choice of job and regiment. His brother described himself as *"Scotch"* on at least one official document. So it seems likely that John Morrison also saw himself as Scottish. After leaving the grammar school John Morrison joined the Clydesdale Bank in Carlisle. It seems likely that he travelled to Quebec, Canada on *"The Virginian"*, arriving June 2 1911 as he joined the Royal Bank of Canada. This has a memorial website, and he is also commemorated on there.

For whatever reason he returned to the UK, and enlisted in Edinburgh on December 17 1914 in the 16th Royal Scots. This battalion was famous as McCrae's Battalion; a volunteer unit formed by Sir George McCrae, who famously marched on to the football pitch at Hearts in Edinburgh leading 500 volunteers. The battalion was notable for its high number of professional sportsmen and fans drawn from football clubs around Scotland.

John was killed on the first day of the battle of the Somme July 1 1916 one of 573 men and 12 officers of the 16th Royal Scots who died that day.

Bernard Arthur Johnson

Dob: September 20 1897

Regt: London

CGS: 1910-13

DoD: May 26 1915

Age: 17

Commemorated: Le Touret Memorial, France

Bernard Arthur Johnson holds the sorry distinction of being the school's youngest casualty of the Great War. He is on the photograph above but we are unsure which boy is Bernard. For a full size image see page 134.

He was the son of Henry and Mary Alice Johnson of 34, Bower Street, Carlisle. His father was a colour sergeant in the Border Regiment, born in India, it seems likely this was a military family. In the 1901 census Bernard was living with his mother and grandparents and three of his aunts in Wandsworth, London. Henry Johnson meanwhile must have been abroad with the army or in barracks.

By the time Bernard was killed his father was already dead and his mother was back in Chelsea where she was born. Had young Bernard been so determined to follow in his father's footsteps that he lied about his age in order to join up? Bernard went to France on March 16 1915 and was killed in the later stages of the Battle of Festubert. In early May 1915 there was a combined French and British operation with the BEF aiming to win control of the Aubers Ridge. When this failed, the Battle of Festubert became, in effect, the second stage of this offensive. The London Regiment took part in this attack and attacked on the evening of May 25 and after 28 hours fighting had suffered five officers killed and three wounded as well as 52 other ranks killed, 252 wounded and 96 missing. Bernard fell during this action. He is commemorated on the Home Office War Memorial as well as on the Le Touret Memorial in Northern France.

Eric William Lafone

Dob: April 19 1896

Regt: DLI

CGS: 1905-06

Dod: June 22 1918

Age: 22

Buried: Granezza British Cemetery Asiago, Italy

Eric William was the eldest son of five children born to the Reverend Henry Pownall Malins Lafone and Gertrude (née Broadbent). After his mother died in 1905, his father married Marion Russell in 1907 and two sons followed.

After school, Eric went up to Cambridge, and later joined the Durham Light Infantry. In 1916 he was fighting on the Somme and was wounded. A telegram on the July 22 1916 reported: *"Regret to inform you that Lt. E.W.Lafone Durham Light Infantry was admitted 14 General Hospital Wimereaux July 19th with gunshot wound and compound fracture of the left arm. Severe, further reports"*. Later Eric was awarded La Croix De Guerre, the French medal for his bravery on July 17 1916 at Pozieres: *"For conspicuous gallantry and devotion to duty, when commanding his company during an attack. He kept them well together under exceptionally trying conditions, when they were suffering heavily from our own guns, but by skilful leading he was able to shift his position and lessen the casualties, afterwards gaining the final objective. His untiring efforts were mainly responsible for the ultimate success of the operation."*

Eric recovered from his injuries and returned to his regiment as captain, fighting in Asiago Italy. Captain Eric Lafone was mentioned in a Despatch from General Plumer dated April 18 1918 and he was also awarded the Military Cross.

It was there in 1918 that he was killed. It seems he went out with a machine gun beyond the wires when the Austrians were pressing a trench to the left. He seems to have mown them down until wounded on the head by a piece of shrapnel. Three men then wanted to fetch him in, but he replied *"Get in yourselves and take the gun, I can crawl in".* While doing so he was caught by a sniper and killed. His Colonel wrote to Eric's father by then an Archdeacon conveying to him the sympathy of every officer and man in his Battalion on the death of his son, who was killed in the early stages of an Austrian attack. He said *"I have looked upon your son as my right hand man...One of the bravest men I have ever met, he was equally loyal to his C.O. and his men. No scheming private could get round him, but he would do anything to serve his men and he was absolutely just: these are his characteristics which never fail to win the hearts of British soldiers, and there is nothing better worth winning. I know the Brigadier and G.O.C. Division share my views. I told him "Lafone is as brave as two tigers" to which he replied "Yes and as gentle as two women". Your boy was a gallant officer because he was a typical gentleman. The sympathy of a stranger can be of no value to you, but the love and respect of 800 brave men has a value. He will be buried tonight in the British Military Cemetery and will lie, as a soldier should beside the men he led and loved. My pioneers are making a cross to mark his grave. I have lost a comrade who might have been my son, but who was in fact my companion in joys and my ready help in troubles".*

Another letter written to the Archdeacon from Cuthbert Vaux second in command to Eric reads—*"When I was wounded Eric was the first person to find and dig me out. On many occasions when shells have burnt in out section I have seen him rush out of the dugout and help wounded men out of trouble. The gallant manner in which he has behaved in the many attacks in which he has taken part. The men loved him and knew that they were safe when under his command. Another incident occurred on the Asiago Plateau Eric took out a reconnoiter patrol of half a dozen men when suddenly a party of some 50 Austrians charged them. Most people would have turned and run but he got his six men down and opened fire at them and broke the group up. This is only one of the many incidents that go to prove his extraordinary character."*

(Research courtesy of Sue Sayers)

William Joseph Cornwall Laurie

DoB: August 13 1884

Regt: Indian Army

CGS: 1894-6

DoD: January 6 1917

A trench at the siege of KUT

Age: 32

Buried: Amara War Cemetery, Iraq

William was born at Monmouth but his father, Donald, a surveyor of taxes, was born in Barbados. His father, William, a sugar merchant, married Leonora Cornwall from Aberdeen. She and Donald had two other sons: George Archibald (who died in Greenock on 1906); and Donald Saunders, OBE, who died of pneumonia in Belgium in 1919. William did his arts degree (including Latin, Greek, Roman history, mathematics, logic and political economy) at the University of Edinburgh and gained a second-class degree. He enrolled at the University of Glasgow in 1905-6 to study political economy, moral philosophy and geology but he did not graduate. He was living at Greenock and it was at this time that his brother died (did this affect his studies?). Sir Henry Jones was Professor of Moral Philosophy and William enrolled in his class and then registered at Christ Church, Oxford in 1907, for one year as an Indian Civil Service Scholar but there is no record of him having taken any exams. While there he made a donation of 245 geological specimens from the Clyde basin below Glasgow to Greenock Philosophical Society.

The Foreign Office catalogue 1912-14 notes that W.J.C. Laurie requested permission to travel from India to Europe via Chinese & Russian Turkestan. As a result of his overland trip back to Britain, which began in May 1914, William wrote an article which appeared in the Journal of the Central Asian Society. He and a companion travelled with 100 baggage *"coolies"* so it was hardly travelling light. Ponies, yaks and camels were also used. The adventure was punctuated by various hunting expeditions, and negotiations with Chinese and Russian dignitaries. He reached London on July 30. It was poignant to read him reporting a narrow escape from Austria following the assassination of Archduke Franz Ferdinand and the Austrian declaration of war against Serbia. He sailed to Bombay from London on October 10 1914 aboard the *Arabia*.

Upon his return to India, in 1914, William joined the 124th Duchess of Connaught's Own Baluchistan Infantry – an Indian Regiment with British officers – which was sent to Persia in 1916. The attack on Kut, under the leadership of Sir Frederick Maude, started on December 13-14 1916. The attack on both sides of the River Tigris took two months just to clear resistance on the west bank below Kut and it was probably during this campaign that William was killed in action in Mesopotamia, on January 6 1917.

Extracts from Laurie's Journal

Five days' marching, at first over a stony plain and then through low and barren sandstone hills, brought us to the Russian frontier post at Irkeshtam. On the way we met and overtook many caravans of camels, ponies, and donkeys. Those going east carried for the most part oil, cloth, and hardware, while wool was the chief article going west. At Irkeshtam a lieutenant of Cossacks was in charge of the customs house, and he had received orders from the Russian Government to pass my baggage. He gave a dinner-party that night, at which two other officers and one of their wives were present.............On July 6 we crossed the Shart Pass, 12,000 feet high, but fairly easy, and entered the basin of the Sir Darya. The Kirghiz in the Alai valley are greedy and disobliging, very different to those on the Taghdumbash Pamir. On the north side of the pass stunted pine-trees were growing, the first we had seen since leaving Kashmir. Three more marches through a cultivated country, in which many Russian monjiku are settled, took us to Osh where I put up in a serai. Our marches after leaving Kashgar had averaged twenty-six miles. Next morning I sold my whole camp equipment, and sent on the other baggage to Andijan in a cart. After parting with Maiyun, I followed in the motor-car which plies between Osh and Andijan. It did the distance of forty miles in two hours. On the following day I left Andijan with Amirullah by the Trans-Caspian Railway, and, after a night in the train, arrived at Samarcand...............The way in which the Russians mix with the inhabitants of the country is very striking. The Turkomans sit at the same tables with Russian officers and ladies in railway refreshment-rooms, and talk, laugh, and smoke, without restraint...........I was lucky to get through Austria, as war was declared on Servia, and the railways were closed on the day after I passed through.

W. J. C. LAURIE.
November 8, 1914.

Cyril Herbert Le Tall

DoB: September 20 1888

Regt: London

CGS: 1902-4

DoD: August 30 1918

Age: 29

Buried: Buissy Cemetery, France

Cyril was the elder son of William Le Tall and his second wife Anne Rebecca Arnold, a prosperous Lincoln family. His grandfather had founded Henry Le Tall Ltd. Henry was born in Yorkshire and presumably business brought him to Lincoln. After leaving school Cyril joined the family business and in 1911 he was living with his cousin Sydney William who also worked in the family business.

Cyril enlisted in the Public School's Battalion, Middlesex Regt on October 26 1914.He received his commission on April 1 1915, and was appointed 2nd Lieutenant in the 16th Service Battalion serving in France. Later he was promoted to Captain in the 1st Battalion of the London Regt. In army records he is described as being 5ft 9 3/4" tall with light brown hair and blue eyes.

In 1918 the battalion was stationed in trenches at Bullecourt engaged in front line fighting. They came under fire from a German counter attack. The commanding officer of the 1st Battalion the London Regt (Royal Fusiliers) Lt. Colonel W R Glover reported to his Colonel on September 16:

"I regret to say that Le Tall was killed in action. From the position in which the bodies were found afterwards he and his men put up a gallant fight during the Bosch counter attack at Bullecourt. It was extraordinary bad luck to be caught just after a relief. He was a very good fellow and will be very much missed".

Otway Trevor MacRitchie Leckie

DoB: August 18 1882

Regt: Indian Army

CGS: 1891-1900

DoD: April 13 1915

Age: 32

Basra Memorial, Iraq

Commemorated: Basra Memorial, Iraq

Otway was the eldest of three sons born to Dr. David Leckie and his wife, Agnes Isabella Kean Brown.
While at school, Otway was captain of the Rugby and cricket teams and he won the senior challenge cup in 1899.

Otway joined the Indian Army and was a captain by 1911. In the war, he joined Wellesley's Rifles which was part of the 6th Poona Division and was sent to Mesopotamia in November 1914. Having captured Basra in 1914, the Poona Division advanced up river in 1915. The Turks fought back and in April opened an attack on Shaiba and Qurna. The website www.firstworldwar.com says *"On 13 April, two days after the bombardment of Shaiba started, Turkish troops attempted to outflank the British across the floods that separated Shaiba from Basra, while Turk cavalry prepared for a frontal assault. However the timely intervention of two British Infantry battalions served to rapidly disperse the Turk cavalry, resulting in a full withdrawal by the latter into woods nearby. Possession of these was in turn secured by the British following an infantry battle throughout 14 April. Casualties during the woodland battle were heavy: the Turks incurred around 2,400 casualties, and the British around half that number. Some 5,000 troops on each side were involved in the fighting in all."* Otway died of his wounds on April 13, 1915 and is commemorated at Basra, Iraq. It is likely he fell in this campaign.

John (Jack) Mitchell Lee

Dob: July 4 1889

Regt: Border

CGS: 1904-08

DoD: September 27 1915

Age: 26

Commemorated: Menin Gate, Belgium

Courtesy of the Lee family

John Mitchell Lee was the middle son of three born to Watson and Jane Lee. His father was a draper at Penrith.

Jack was a keen sportsman and won the school medal for sport in 1908. He played in the school Rugby and football teams. He graduated from Cambridge University with first class honours in chemistry in 1910. When war broke out he was working for chemical manufacturers in Birmingham.

Jack had been in the trenches about five weeks when he was killed in an attack on the enemy trenches, an action for which he had volunteered. Lieutenant Howard Morgan of the 7th Battalion Border Regiment reported: *"he probably held the Germans for two hours alone, when he was severely wounded in the back. He was bandaged and placed in a German dug-out by his three men. Eventually the Germans turned their artillery on to their own trench which we had taken, and shelled us out. One of the bombers reported that a shell had dropped on the dug-out in which Mr Lee was lying. This is all we can gather of what happened... Jack...was one of the bravest men I ever knew. He scoffed at bullets and shells. He undertook some of the most hazardous tasks, and was respected and loved by officers and men alike."*

His Commanding Officer wrote: *"He showed the greatest courage and devotion to duty; his gallantry is a great source of pride to us all..."*

Charles Reeves Liddell

DoB: May 14 1892

Regt: Royal Field Artillery

CGS: 1905-07

DoD: April 21 1918

Age: 25

Laying a field telephone line, WW1

Buried: Bienvillers Military Cemetery, France

Charles was born in Manchester when his father, Charles Isaac, was there working with his brother-in-law, WH Reeves. His parents were from Cumbria and moved back to Stanwix. Charles became a draughtsman with Messrs. Cowan, Sheldon and Co., and worked there for about eight years.

Charles enlisted in early September 1914 as a gunner in the Royal Field Artillery and he saw fighting on different war fronts,serving for six months in Gallipoli and 12 months in Egypt, and then to France for about 14months. He was gassed in September 1917and after a couple of months in hospital he was attached to another field battery. Later he transferred back to his original battery.

Major WT Higbst(?) wrote: *"He was killed by a shell whilst repairing a telephone line near the Battery position this morning. His death would be instantaneous. The fact that he died bravely doing his duty and that his end came without pain or suffering may be to you as it is to us his comrades...some small fragment of consolation in your grief...A general favourite in the battery he was in every sense of the word a real soldier, as fearless as he was modest. His particular work – a lineman – is at times dangerous and calls for a high standard of personal courage and endurance. Never has your son been known to hesitate or fail in his duty or to shrink from any personal danger. His work, always done in a quiet and unassuming way, was invariably thoroughly and conscientiously done, and it can be truly be said of him that no one who has given his all to his* country and his country's cause has served more faithfully than he. I know that Colonel Mason…had the very highest opinion of your son's sterling qualities. As a soldier and as a comrade, the battery is poorer by his death. I am sending his body down to the back area tonight, and it will be laid to rest in the British cemetery at —————- tomorrow."

Colonel Mason wrote to say: "Charlie…(has) been awarded the Military Medal for a specific act of bravery in the field…Alas! That your poor boy, whom I know so well, is not here for me to convey to him personally my congratulations. He was one of my most trusted men whose technical knowledge was invaluable – a charming personality, modest and unassuming to such a degree as to be a stumbling block to his own advancement. His duty was a dangerous one; and so keen was he always that communications should be maintained that he never spared himself – on occasions, indeed, he had to be restrained from going out, so great was the risk to himself. England need never fear so long as she can produce such men as he – the personification of unselfishness and self-sacrifice. He realised the vital importance of his work and he did it honestly and fearlessly. Great and cruel though I know the blow of his death will be to you…yet be thankful for a son who was a good soldier and a good man. His life, I am sure, has not been lived in vain."

Trinity school pupils and staff walking along the line of a First World War trench at Newfoudland Park, Beaumont-Hamel on the Somme.

78

William Keir Little

Dob: July 30 1879

Regt: London

CGS: 1892-96

DoD: October 5 1916

Age: 37

Thiepval Memorial, the Somme

Commemorated: Thiepval Memorial, France

William was the elder son of William and Jane M Church. Keir was his maternal grandmother's name. The family originated in Scotland and in 1881 they were living in Dumfriesshire where William's father farmed 4 000 acres and employed four men and a boy. By 1891 Jane was a widow and living in Carlisle. William had older half-sisters, Jane Mary, Christian [sic] and Eleanor, whom his father had with his first wife, Jane Margaret Cochrane, who died in 1873 of TB. Agnes Hepburn was his older sister, and his younger siblings were Elliot and Norah. In 1901 Mrs Little was living on Petteril Street with Agnes and Norah and by 1911 she and Agnes had moved to Melcombe Regis.

William enlisted at Battersea into the 13th County of London Battalion (Princess Louise's Kensington Battlion). He was living in Kilburn, London in 1911. From February 11 1916, the Battalion transferred to the 168th Brigade in 56th (London) Division. The 56th was involved in every part of the Battle of the Somme. Following the Battle of Morval (September 25-27) the 56th Division relieved the Guards Division and the 6th Division in the region of Les Boeufs.

William was killed between this date and the Battle of the Transloy Ridges (October 7-20). The attack had been due to start on October 5 but was postponed due to bad weather. The bombardment opened up therefore on October 6, with the assault itself beginning the day after. As William died on October 5, it is clear casualties were taking place throughout this period.

Malcolm Macdonald

DoB: June 30 1897

Regt: Argyll and Sutherland Highlanders

CGS: 1907-15

DoD: October 13 1916

Age: 19

Commemorated: Thiepval Memorial, France

Thanks to the MacDonald family for the photograph

Malcolm was the elder son of Dr James Macdonald and his wife Gertrude Lucy. James hailed from Edinburgh and Gertrude from Carlisle. Malcolm went to the University of Edinburgh as a medical student before joining up. He had a brother Iain, also a student of CGS (1910-1916) and Edinburgh, who became a doctor, and having been captured at Singapore in the Second World War, served in the camps on the Burmese railway.

Malcolm had joined up at the earliest possible age, choosing his own regiment, and training in Scotland. *"He entered with great ardour into his military duties, and his recommendations for a commission in the Border Regiment only awaited the formal ratification of his Colonel at the time of his death."*

The Cumberland News reported that a letter of October 27th sent to a friend of the family from a Sergeant of Malcolm's platoon read: *"Malcolm...was on a ration party to the front line, and they were not long returned and had gone into a shelter for a sleep...the Hun sent over one of his big shells, which landed in the bay where Malcolm was sleeping, and it killed him, and a chum, Private Woodrow...When I heard the shell burst I jumped to see what was the matter and poor Malcolm was gone. Malcolm was a true soldier, and brave, and I have much sympathy with you in your sad bereavement. It nearly made me cry to lose him, because he was such a willing lad, and it was also his first turn in the trenches."*

John Mitchell Mackay

DoB: August 1 1879

Regt: Royal Engineers

CGS: 1893

DoD: August 10 1917

Age: 38

Buried: Hooge Crater Cemetery, Belgium

John was the middle son of George and Isabella Mackay both from Scotland. George Mackay was Chief Constable of the city and the family's address was the Police Office, West Walls. Isabella died in 1883 aged 28 leaving her three little sons aged three, four and five motherless. All three boys attended the Grammar School.

By 1901 John was in London working as a civil engineer. Later he went to India to work for the Public Works Department in Bombay. His brothers Alexander and George both emigrated to Canada and enlisted in the CEF in 1915. Both survived the war.

On the outbreak of war, John volunteered at once, but the Government of India was unable to release him from his work. He came home on leave in April 1916 and obtained permission from the India Office to join the army. He was granted a commission in the Royal Engineers – East Kent Regiment 19984 – and went on active service in January 1917.

John was killed in August 1917 at Ypres. Despite enquiries from his family, no details surrounding the circumstances of his death were available. He was reburied in 1920 from his original site south east of Westhoeck, Ypres, to Hooge Crater.

Walter Maxwell

DoB: January 17 1893

Regt: South Wales Borderers

CGS: 1903-7

DoD: February 11 1918

Age: 25

Bangalore Military Cemetery

Buried: Bangalore (Hosur Road) Cemetery, India

Walter was born in Bankhead Canonbie, Roxburghshire, the son of William Frank and Mary Maxwell. His father came from Bewcastle, and his mother from KirkAndrews-on-Esk. In 1911 Walter was living with his mother on Scotland Road, Stanwix, Carlisle and he was an apprentice livestock auctioneer.

Although the record says that Walter served with the 1st Battalion South Wales Borderers, on the date he died they were fighting on the Western Front around the area of Langemark in Belgium and Walter died of heart failure at Mhow Station in India.

Captain Cockcroft wrote: *"He came into my company in September 1917, and we at once became great friends...He was a most reliable, keen young officer, and had a great command of men. No day was too long for him. My men loved him, and it was the greatest shock, and to me to hear of his death at Bangalore. ...we have lost a great friend."* Captain MF Thomas said: *"I had formed the highest of him. He was a very good officer, keen on his work, and a more willing and obliging man I have seldom met...He was very popular with his brother officers and he will be much missed by us all. He has done his duty well and he has given for his King and country quite as much as if he had been killed in action."* A fellow officer A T Nicholson said Maxwell: *"was recognised as an authority in his special line of signalling and he will be greatly missed."*

Herbert Curry McCumiskey

DoB: November 20 1891

Regt: Border

CGS: 1906-8

DoD: November 21 1915

Age: 24

Commemorated: Basra Memorial, Iraq.

Thanks to the McCumiskey family for the photograph

Herbert was the youngest son of Patrick McCumiskey, who was from Dromintee in Ireland, and Charlotte Hudson of Carlisle. Patrick was a marine store dealer, with premises on Collier Lane. The 1882 Cumberland Directory describes the business as *"wholesale and retail dealers in rags, ropes, scrap iron and all kinds of old metals, skins and glass bottles"*. In 1909 they moved to the Crown Works on Crown Street a big five storey building. They must have done well, as there is a record of Herbert going to Canada in 1912 on a business trip; possibly to do with the skins (ie furs) they dealt in. Before the war however, Herbert was working as a bank clerk in the London Joint City and Midland Bank, Carlisle. The 1/4thCumberland and Westmorland Battalion arrived in India in December 1914. In August 1915, a detachment under Lt Wilson was sent to Mesopotamia for service. Herbert was part of this small detachment that transferred to the Persian Gulf.

Herbert died in 1915, (the day after his birthday) of beri-beri and jaundice, whilst in Mesopotamia (now modern day Iraq). A memorial service was held for Herbert at Carlisle's Lowther Street Congregational Church. The Rev. Edward Booth said that from Private McCumiskey *"no complaint was ever penned, and never did he wince. Bravely did he endure, bravely did he face the foe, and bravely did he die."*

George McPherson

DoB: June 7 1887

Regt: DLI

CGS: 1905-6

DoD: September 16 1916

Age: 29

Buried: Flers, France

Coxhoe Church school
George is one of the two young teachers
seen at both ends of the photograph.
We are not sure which one is George.

George was the youngest child of William McPherson and his second wife Jane Little. William was born in Aberdeenshire but was living at Longtown by 1861. William worked on the railway his whole life starting as a labourer and ending as a "railway permanent way inspector", this post meant that he had responsibility for a particular stretch of railway and the embankments alongside. William's first wife died 1n 1871 leaving him with four young children. He married George's mother Jane in 1877, and they had four sons John, William, James and George. Jane's family came from just over the border at Canonbie; her father had a small farm of thirty acres. George attended the Grammar School from 1905 to 1906 and he was in the pupil teacher's class along with Arthur Hetherington and the brothers of Reginald Atkinson and James Batey.

After leaving the Grammar School he attended Bede College Durham and went on to take up a post as assistant master at Coxhoe Church School, Coxhoe. George enlisted just days after war was declared on August 31 1914 at Stockton-on-Tees. On his attestation papers George was described as 5ft 9" tall with a good physical physique. He landed in France on April 17 1915. The 15th battalion Durham Light Infantry (DLI) arrived months later so George must have been in another unit and transferred later to the 15th. The 1/6th and 1/7th of the DLI both arrived in France in mid April so he may well have been with them.

The 15th Battalion Durham Light Infantry (DLI) was part of the 64th Division and fought at Loos and the Somme. The battle of Flers-Courcelette began on September 15. George McPherson was part of B company. The 15th DLI began to move at 2am and marched to Flers. They advanced at 8.45 am but by 10am

84

they were pinned down in shell holes and remained there until dusk when they withdrew to Flea Trench. The battalion was relieved by the 20th battalion DLI the next day. The DLI war diary listed George as missing on September 17. He was one of 209 other ranks who died during September 16/17. This battle marked the first use of tanks.

George's brother William wrote on behalf of their widowed mother the following month asking for further information. George was later declared dead and his grave was located. His personal possessions were not returned to the family until July 1920. George is also commemorated on Coxhoe village war memorial, Longtown war memorial and the family memorial in Arthuret Churchyard, Longtown. George's brother William married James Herbert Batey's sister Alice. James died in 1915.

The Legend of the Basilica at Albert

During the early days of the war German artillery had shelled the Basilica, trying to knock it down and prevent the French artillery spotters from using it. They had only succeeded in dislodging the statue of Mary, which by 1916 hung at a precarious angle just below the horizontal. This was just too visible and too heavenly-connected for the soldiers passing through the town. The Legend of the Leaning [or Hanging] Virgin was born.

The British rendition was that whoever knocked her down would lose the war, the Germans apparently believing the opposite. Another version of the legend had it that the fall of the Virgin

would signal the end of the war. The details of the various versions seem secondary to the belief by troops of all sides that the Virgin's natural descent was halted temporarily by a Divine Hand so its final destruction could mark the War's end.

It must have provided a double psychic reassurance that the Forces of Heaven had taken an interest in protecting the Virgin and her Child and would eventually take steps to end the suffering on the battlefield.

Courtesy of David Ramshaw

Thomas Hindson Mellish

DoB: September 5 1894

Regt: Royal Scots

CGS: 1909-13

DoD: October 22 1917

Age: 23

Commemorated: Tyne Cot Memorial, Belgium

Thomas was the only son of William Mellish and Sarah Hindson. He had a younger sister Evelyn Mary. William was a railwayman – a platform inspector in 1901 and 1911 – and Assistant Stationmaster in 1917. He was the son of a farm labourer and was born in Sebergham. Sarah was the daughter of a stonemason from Lazonby. According to Thomas' attestation papers the family was Wesleyan. At the time of Thomas' death they were living at Station House, Halifax.

Thomas was educated at Brook Street School followed by Carlisle Grammar School from 1909 – 1913. He was captain of the football team and was also in the school cricket team in 1913. After leaving the Grammar School he became an assistant master at Ashley Street Boys School.

Shortly after the outbreak of war, Thomas volunteered for service with the Argyll and Sutherland Highlanders and was transferred to the Royal Scots in September 1917. He received instruction in York and qualified in muskets, physical drill, bayonet training, squad drill and rifle exercises. He spent much of the war in the UK, as an instructor. Such was the shortage of NCOs, however, that he was sent to one of the platoons in C Company as platoon sergeant.

On the night of 20/21 October 1917 the 16th Battalion Royal Scots was in the Salient as part of the 3rd Battle of Ypres known as Passchendaele. They went into the front line just to the north of Poelcapelle *"After the usual dreary sojourn in the depressing camps near Ypres"* they were *"buffeted by shell fire on the way".* The attack was to be launched on the 22nd at 5.35am, the 15th and 16th Royal Scots being the leading battalions but the task given them was *"difficult and complicated"* said John Ewing in the Royal Scots. *"The water-logged nature of the country rendered the punctual assembly of the troops a very anxious business. The men could scarcely drag themselves through the mud, and the Boches added to their misery by putting down a savage barrage along the assembly positions, causing many casualties and throwing the troops into confusion. But the excellent leadership of the officers and NCOs and the discipline of the men triumphed...The 22nd October was probably the most ghastly day experienced by the 15th and the 16th Royal Scots...the latter (lost) twelve officers and 244 other ranks in killed, wounded and missing...For their failure the Royal Scots were in no sense to blame: the conditions which they had to endure were such that it was not in mortals to command success".*

Captain Sutherland wrote to Thomas' father: *"Your son was hit by a piece of shell about 1am, a few hours previous to moving into a position for attack. I had him taken into an old German 'pill-box' and attended to as best we could, but he was rendered unconscious from the first. About midday on the 22nd I myself got back wounded to the same 'pill-box' and was told that Sergeant Mellish had just died. I had a very high opinion of your son, and he was held in the highest esteem by the officers and men of his company. He was my most reliable N.C.O. and I noticed that his moral qualities had a great effect upon his men."*

The Cumberland News also reported that of 25 Carlisle teachers who had volunteered for service: *"Sergeant Mellish is the first to pay the supreme sacrifice for the defence of those at home."* The news of his death was greeted with great sorrow by the staff and students at Ashley School: *"with whom his fine personal qualities made him very popular"* and the school flag was displayed at half-mast.

George Norman

DoB: March 9 1890

Regt: NZEF

CGS: 1904 - 5

DoD: October 12 1917

Age: 27

Commemorated: Tyne Cot, Belgium

Great Orton War Memorial

George was the eldest of five sons born to Thomas and Jane Norman. The Norman family had been farming at Bow, near Great Orton for generations. He attended the Grammar School for two years and then worked on the family farm.

George travelled to New Zealand in 1912 and after war broke out he joined the 3rd Otago Regt. New Zealand Expeditionary Force and died in the First Battle of Passchendaele on October 12 1917. Nearly 3,000 New Zealanders died or were injured that day. It remains the worst day in New Zealand's military history.

George was not the first member of his family to visit New Zealand. His father Thomas Blaylock Norman had been there in the mid 1880's prior to his marriage to George's mother in 1889. He had stayed there long enough to be listed on the electoral roll. So whether George was planning to make New Zealand his permanent home is not known.

George is also commemorated on the village war memorial in the churchyard at Great Orton. One of the other eight names is that of the Rector's son Richard Parker Gilbanks, who also attended the Grammar School.

George's second cousin Robert Mayson Calvert, is also commemorated on the school memorial. Both were the great-grandsons of George and Elizabeth Blaylock.

Max Ogilvy-Ramsay

DoB: June 5 1893

RFC

CGS: 1907-12

DoD: August 4 1918

Age: 25

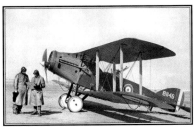
Bristol Aeroplane

Buried: Montecchio Precalcino Communal Cemetery Extension, Italy.

Max was the son of Dr Maxwell and Isabella Ogilvy-Ramsay. He had a sister, Mary, and the 1901 and 1911 Census list both Mary and Max living with their parents at Portland Square, Carlisle.

Max joined the Royal Flying Corps and was commissioned as a 2nd Lieutenant on June 7 1917. He was appointed Flying Officer (Pilot) on August 11 1917.

He was the pilot of a Bristol F2b bomber, serial number D8081, accompanied by 2nd Lieut Frank Frewin Crump, RAF as gunner/ observer when he left Villaverla aerodrome, Italy at 2.40pm on August 1 1918. He was in combat with enemy aircraft and was forced to land and crashed on Italian Grossa aerodrome at 3.00pm. The aircraft was damaged and both pilot and observer were injured.

Max died of his injuries on August 4 1918 aged 20.

Head of History Linda Hodgson with pupils at the Menin Gate.

Christopher Edward Parker

DoB: June 14 1880

Regt: Royal Artillery

CGS: 1892-6

DoD: February 27 1917

Age: 36

Buried: Rugeley Cemetery, Staffordshire, UK

Christopher was the eldest son of John Knubley Parker, a Justice of the Peace from Caldbeck, and Caroline Parker, from Ousby, Cumberland. They lived at Evening Hill, Thursby, after marrying in 1879 in Westmoreland. Christopher seems to have been named after both his Grandfather and Great Grandfather. A second son, John Henry Francis Parker was born in 1882, and a third son, Cecil Newland, in 1886.

Christopher was a bank clerk before he joined up.

He died at Rugeley Training Camp, of acute septic bronchitis, aged 36.

Trinity School pupils Ruth Cox, Rebecca Morley, Alexandra Jefferson, Steven Barker and Alex Graham laying a wreath at the Menin gate on behalf of the school.

90

James Dowell Parkin

DoB: March 11 1895

Regt: DLI

CGS: 1910

DoD: March 27 1918

Age: 23

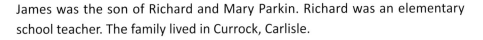

Commemorated: Soisssons Memorial, France

James was the son of Richard and Mary Parkin. Richard was an elementary school teacher. The family lived in Currock, Carlisle.

James joined up in December 1915 when he was working as a clerk for Cumberland County Council. He went to France on April 15 1918 after being gazetted. It is unclear whether this was his first time in action.

He died of wounds received near Bouffignereux, France. There was fierce fighting in the area near Soissons on May 27 (the Battle of the Aisne) in which the 1st Wiltshire Battalion, as part of the 25th Division (7th Brigade) was involved.

James disappeared in this action and for the next year, his father sent letters to the Military Secretary, asking about his son: *"as it is now nearly seven weeks since we are all very anxious..."* The letters are very poignant. He asks if it is possible that James has lost his memory due to shell shock; or whether he can be a prisoner-of-war in Germany. In one letter Richard Parkin describes his son: *"was about 5ft 11in in height, has a slight scar on left cheek opposite the corners of the mouth (from a cut)...eyes dark blue; hair dark brown. Limbs exceptionally large and muscular. Sings remarkably well – favourites classical pieces - church music. Voice – baritone."* In 1919 the authorities declared: *"A thorough search was made throughout all the hospitals and prisoner of war camps in Germany and no trace of Second Lieutenant Parkin could be found."*

James Bruce Pearson

DoB: 18 August 1889

Regt: Indian Army

CGS: 1901-07

DoD: 5 March 1917

Age: 27

Commemorated: Basra Memorial, Iraq

James was the fifth child of James and Maria Pearson. His father's family were from Carlisle but his mother came from Scotland.

James enjoyed sport at school: he played in the Rugby, football and cricket teams. The Cumberland News reported he was: *"very popular in Carlisle, especially in Rugby football circles, and he had played for Carlisle and Cumberland."*

There is some confusion over James's date of death. He probably arrived in Mesopotamia in August 1915 as part of a small detachment under the command of Lt. AP Wilson. In the obituary in the local paper of June 23 1917, it is stated that James was reported missing on March 15. His father received a letter from Major HL Houghton dated April 14 stating that the force had attacked the enemy but their position was *"untenable"* and they had to retire. *"Your son was with one of the companies in rear, and behaved with great gallantry throughout"* and it was not possible to see exactly what had happened but *"I feel sure your son must have died gallantly while holding up the enemy to cover the retirement of his party...I am afraid I can offer small hope of his being a prisoner as we should most likely have heard of it by now, and the fighting is so fierce that few prisoners are generally captured on either side."*

Henry Allason Mason Peile

DoB: January 7 1896

Regt: London Rifle Brigade.

CGS: 1906-7

DoD: July 1 1916

Age: 20

Commemorated: Thiepval Memorial, France

Grave of
unknown soldiers

Henry was the son of Walker Peile and Gertrude Simpson, of 7 St. James' Road, Carlisle. His father was recorded as a grocer's assistant in 1891 and a commission agent in 1901. He died in 1909. In the 1911 Census Henry is recorded as being a boarder at the Friends School, Wigton.

Henry enlisted into the 3rd Battalion London Rifle Brigade in early 1915 and went to France in a draft to the 1st Battalion in October of that year. He was part of the 56th Division which formed in February 1916. The London Rifle Brigade was quite exclusive – demanding an entry fee – and so attracted the more privileged classes. In May and June they were training behind the lines at Arras. The 56th Division was ordered to attack at Gommecourt on the first day of the Battle of the Somme, July 1, 1916. The width of No-Man's Land was perhaps 800 yards in May – too far for the troops to cross – and time was spent extending the trenches although bad weather in June hampered progress. The distance on July 1 was still between 250 and 400 yards however. The riflemen crossed No-Man's Land at a walk, as ordered, but were cut down by machine gun fire. By 8.30pm the surviving men of the Division were given the order *"every man for himself"* and they tried to get back to the British lines. The two divisions at Gommecourt suffered 6,769 casualties, of whom 2,206 men were killed. Gommecourt was not taken. More than 300 London Rifle Brigade men were killed on that day, or died from wounds later. Henry was reported wounded and missing; and officially reported killed in action.

John Scott

DoB: March 29 1894

Regt: DLI

CGS: 1906-8

DoD: March 27 1918

Age: 23

Commemorated: Pozieres Memorial, France

John was the son of Joseph Scott, a solicitor and in the 1911 Census was aged 17 and living at home in Welcome Square, Scotby, with his mother Mary Jane, and brothers, Stewart (18) and Tom Conway (12). He was already working as a clerk on the London and North Western Railway.

The family seem to have originated in Cumbria: Grandfather John Scott was a provision dealer from Rockcliffe.

John joined the Durham Light Infantry in 1915; and was made 2nd Lieutenant in 1917. The 22nd Battalion became part of the 8th Division in July 1916.

Pozieres was a German stronghold on the main Albert-Bapaume road which was only won after prolonged fighting and considerable cost during the Battle of the Somme in 1916. During the German Spring Offensive of March 1918 however, Pozieres was recaptured on the 24/25 March. The 8th Division was part of the Fifth Army which took part in the Battle of St Quentin, and the actions at the Somme crossings at this time. As John died of wounds on March 27 1918, it seems likely he was wounded during the German attack. The Germans advanced some 40 miles and the British and Commonwealth casualties, dead, wounded and missing, numbered more than 177,000. The German army also suffered heavy losses.

William Dalton Columbo Sharp

Dob: April 17 1882

Regt: Norfolk

CGS: 1895-98

DoD: October 9 1917

Age: 35   -

Thanks to the Sharp family for the photograph

Commemorated: Tyne Cot Memorial, Belgium

William had the unusual distinction of having been born at sea, aboard the ship Columbo (in the Indian Ocean), hence his name. Two of his siblings were also born on the Columbo. There were also four other siblings, who were all born at Bowness-on-Solway like their father Johnston Sharp. He became a Ship Master and by 1901 was retired and living at Aglionby Street, Carlisle. His mother Margaret originated in Scotland.
William played in the Rugby team for the school in 1897.

He was an articled clerk in Carlisle in 1901, but by 1911 he was living at Parsons Green, Fulham, as a chartered accountant.

Many Londoners joined the Norfolk Regiment. The 1st Battalion, Norfolk Regiment fought at the Battle of Poelcapelle, one of the series referred to as Third Ypres or Passchendaele. The 15 Brigade attacked with the 1st Norfolks and the 16th R. Warwicks. Moving forward at 5.20am they were checked by fire from Polderhoek Chateau and supporting pillboxes. Fire and the mud stopped any real progress being made and the troops were forced back to their original position. Another attack scheduled for that night was cancelled.

William was killed in action; one of 45 soldiers from this Battalion who died on that day.

Douglas Alexander Mackay Shepherd

DoB: December 12 1890

Regt: London

CGS: 1901-10

DoD: September 19 1916

Age: 25

Buried: Combles Community Cemetery Extension, France

Douglas was the sixth of seven sons born to Canon William Mutrie Shepherd, Vicar of St John's, Carlisle.Three of his brothers also attended the Grammar School (of these, two served in the War and survived).

Douglas was excellent at sport and was in the Rugby, cricket and football teams, captaining cricket and Rugby. He won the senior challenge cup in 1910. Douglas went up to Queen's College, Oxford. His provost reported that Douglas was: *"healthy & strong, played cricket and football, didn't debate much, can sing & play the piano, hopes to be a schoolmaster."* In 1912 he matriculated with a fourth class in honour classical moderations and in 1914 a third class in the final honour school of modern history but did not supplicate for a degree. After leaving College he became an assistant master at Cranbrook , Kent.

Douglas joined the University Contingent of the OTC and enlisted in 1916. He served with 16th Battalion London (Queen's Westminster Rifles).

He was only in France for a short time before he was killed in action on the Somme in September near Leuze Wood. This was during the second phase of the Battle of the Somme. On September 4 the Germans had launched a counter-attack on the newly won British position near Mouquet Farm (commonly known as Mucky Farm), but were repulsed by the Australians. There was significant fighting in the area during the following three weeks.

Henry Lamont Simpson

DoB: June 5 1897

Regt: Lancashire Fusiliers

CGS: 1908-1916

DoD: August 29 1918

Age: 21

Commemorated: Vis-en-Artois Memorial, France

Courtesy Carlisle Library

Henry was the eldest of four children born to Henry Colbeck Simpson and Margaret Jane (née Quirk). Henry senior was a tailor and hosier (employer) from Newcastle, according to the 1901 Census. Mother Margaret was born in India but her mother, Matilda, was from the Isle of Man. The 1891 Census show her living in Warwick Square, Carlisle, a school mistress. Interestingly, in 1881, when a pupil teacher, she was living with her mother and uncle Richard Carson, a Chelsea Pensioner, who had served in the British Army between 1860 and 1878, so there was clearly a family history of military service.

Henry appears to have been academic. He was awarded a maths prize in 1909 and junior classics prize in 1911. He was awarded the school medal (sports) 1914. He played Smike in Nicholas Nickleby. By 1913 he was a prefect and librarian and took prizes in reading, French and maths. In 1914 he was house captain and was very active in the dramatic productions; playing the lead in "Ivanhoe" and appearing with Hannay in a comedy *"French as he is spoke"*. He won the Chancellor's medal, the literature prize and maths prize (again!). Henry was active also in the debating society. *"HL Simpson is one of the best speakers we have this term, his speeches are generally a pleasure to listen to, both on account of his original ideas, the excellent way he delivers them and a delightful vein of humour never lacking".* He opposed the motion that "the construction of a Channel Tunnel is unadvisable" and recommended having theatres and hotels at the bottom of the sea "where the fishes might see our beauty". In 1915 Henry was the editor of the Carliol and school captain.

He was good at sport too: we have a photo of him in the school cricket team from 1913 and he played in the Rugby XV 1915 *("useful in the scrum")*. He was also tennis captain.

Henry won a scholarship to Cambridge, but deferred going up to university in favour of joining up. The 8th Battalion Lancashire Fusiliers had been at Gallipoli and Egypt, but from February 1917 had transferred to the Western Front. Henry received his commission to the Lancashire Fusiliers on June 26 1917. On September 6, the War Diary records that HL Simpson had been wounded, and while he had joined the 1/8th in France, he was actually in Belgium when he was injured. It was bad timing as the Battalion was relieved the next day and retired to camp at Brandhoek. At some point Henry returned to the front, this time in the 1st Battalion. The Lancashire Fusiliers 1918 Annual reported that: *"On the 29th the Intelligence Officer, 2/Lieut. H.L. Simpson was killed while reconnoitering "No Man's Land."* According to the preface of his book of poetry, he was killed by a sniper's bullet.

There is a short letter from his father to the Master of Pembroke, Cambridge from September 25 which reads: *"It is my painful duty to notify you that my son 2nd Lieut, HL Simpson, for whom you were holding a scholarship, was killed in action in France on August 28th* (sic)*".*

In 1919, Henry's former English teacher H. C. Duffin, who taught at the school from 1912-16, published Henry's poems in a book *"Mood and Tenses"*. In the introductory remarks, Duffin says of his pupil: *"His spirit was fine, swift, vivacious and at the same time firm-set in sanity and strength"*. There are 40 items in the book, mainly poems with a couple of prose sections. The dates of the poems range from 1914 to 1918, which suggests that some were written whilst he was still at school and others at the front. In the poem "The Wine-Cellar", it is touching to read his reminisces of School while he is at war:

"In the Sixth, at School,
When the world was largely a joke,
And we were learning to play the fool
In half a hundred happy ways".

William Sinclair

DoB: September 29 1897

Regt: Manchester

CGS: 1910-13

DoD: September 11 1917

Age: 19

Commemorated: Tyne Cot Memorial, Belgium

William was the son of William and Jane Sinclair of Lanarkshire, Scotland. His father was a railway clerk from Govan; and later a railway parcels agent in Carlisle. While at school, William played for the cricket team.

He is recorded as having enlisted in Carlisle but it is unclear when. The Carlisle Grammar School Register records William as belonging to the London Regiment; however he was killed while serving with 1st/9th Battalion, Manchester Regiment. The 1/9th Battalion of the Manchester Regiment was in France from March 1917.

As William is commemorated at the Tyne Cot Memorial, he was clearly involved in the 3rd Battle of Ypres (later known as Passchendaele). John Hartley, writing about the activities of the Manchester Battalion on 11 September reported: *"The History of 42nd Division has them attacking an enemy blockhouse."* And he included a quote from the divisional history: *"Private T M Howard, 9th Manchester, volunteered to bring in an officer who lay wounded about 40 yards from the blockhouse, from which severe machine gun and rifle fire was maintained. Howard reached the officer and carried him 200 yards over exposed ground illuminated by enemy flares."* John Hartley added: *"The attack had obviously failed."*

Frank Bousfield Somerville

Dob: March 8 1897

Navy: Royal

CGS: 1906-12

DoD: January 1 1915

Age: 17

HMS Formidable

Commemorated: Chatham Naval Memorial, UK

Frank was the second child of seven born to Michael B. Somerville and Mary Elizabeth Somerville. Michael Somerville was a commercial traveller in the flour trade.

Frank was on a training ship in the Mersey after leaving school and had joined *HMS Formidable* in August 1914. He was one of 600 men lost on New Year's Day 1915 when a German submarine, U24, torpedoed his ship, *HMS Formidable,* which was the first British battleship sunk in the First World War. The Fleet had been on manoeuvres on 31 December and had gone over the same area of sea in so doing. It was a clear night with a full moon, so had proved an easy target for the U boat. As *HMS Formidable* was the last in line she became the one attacked. Commander KGB Dewar on board *HMS Prince of Wales* later wrote that hostile ships should have been expected in the area and as this was simply an exercise such a risk should not have been taken.

Of the 747 men on *HMS Formidable*, 34 Officers and 513 ratings died. They were either blown up by the torpedo attack, had drowned, or died of exposure. Of these only 18 bodies were recovered. Frank's body was not one of them. The Cumberland News reported Frank's death (*"A promising young Carlisle lad"*) on January 9 1915 and revealed two other men on board from Carlisle had been saved. Frank's family had actually received a card from him on New Year's Day.

Kenneth James Stafford

DoB: April 7 1898

Regt: Royal Field Artillery

CGS: 1908-9

DoD: November 14 1918

Age: 20

Field hospital

Buried: St. Sever Cemetery Extension, Rouen, France

Kenneth was the only son of John Owen Stafford and his wife Mary Anne Smith Tweedie Kerr. He had two sisters. At the time of Kenneth's death his father was the minister at Gretna, the family's address was "The Manse", Gretna. Kenneth's paternal grandfather had been a school teacher in Scotland and his maternal grandfather was a wire manufacturer in Cheshire. However he too was a Scot by birth. After attending the Grammar School, Kenneth went to Clifton Bank School, St. Andrews and Edinburgh University.

Kenneth enlisted in Edinburgh on April 19 1916. He applied for a commission on September 8 1916. He is described as 5ft 6 1/2" and he weighed 124lbs, He stated that he'd had artillery experience in the Edinburgh University O.T.C. He was mobilised one month later on October 26 1916. He was promoted to 2nd lieutenant in the R.F.A. (Special Reserve) on February 20 1917. Just over a year later he was promoted to lieutenant on August 20 1918, although the notice of the promotion did not appear in the London Gazette until the day he died. He injured his left thumb on September 1 1918, and his family were sent a telegram. Two months later on November 8 they received a second telegram stating,

"Regret Lieutenant K J Stafford RFA 37th Battery admitted 8th General Hospital Rouen. Dangerously ill gunshot wound left ear, temple penetrated, left arm compound fracture. Further news sent immediate. Visit not possible."

A further telegram was received a week later on November 15:

"Deeply regret Lieutenant K J Stafford RFA died of wounds"

He was posthumously awarded the Military Cross. His citation in the London Gazette stated:

"Lt. Kenneth James Stafford R.F.A. (Spec. Res.), attd. 37th By., 27th Bde. For great gallantry and devotion to duty on 4th November, 1918, near Beaudignies, when his battery was very heavily shelled. he went up to the position and remained there for some hours, encouraging the men and attending to several who were wounded. He continued to do so after being badly wounded. Throughout these operations he has set a fine example to those with him."

Pupils and staff take a rest on their battlefield visit to Newfoundland Park,
Beaumont-Hamel on the Somme

Thomas William Stanfield

Dob: December 20 1890

Regt: Yorkshire

CGS: 1906-10

Dod: November 23 1917

Age: 26

Buried: Anneux British Cemetery, France

Thomas was the son of George and Janet Stanfield. His father, originally from Levenshulme, was a boiler and engine fitter. His mother (née Armstrong) was from Scotland and he had older sisters, Elizabeth, Mary Annie, Lena, and Margaret Isabella and a brother, George.

On the outbreak of war, Thomas was a school teacher. He had also spent two earlier years in the Hampshire Regiment. He was initially a private in the Durham Light Infantry, joining up in October 1914. He was sometimes disobedient, three misdemeanours were recorded in November 1914, being absent from tattoo; reveille; and church parade.

Thomas was in Egypt between December 1915 and March 1916 when he transferred to France. In 1916 he was awarded the Military Medal for *"carrying an important message through shell fire"*. It appears he was also wounded in France on July 26 1916, and arrived in hospital in Nottingham in August 1916. After receiving his commission, he joined the Yorkshire Regiment.

Thomas was serving with the 13th Battalion in November 1917, when he and the battalion marched up to Beaumetz-les-Cambrais and from there moved into captured German trenches near Graincourt. On November 23, Thomas and his men followed the tanks as they advanced towards their objective of Bourlon Wood and village. There was fierce fighting and by 3pm the Germans had given up on the position but had responded with a heavy bombardment.

The Cumberland News reported Thomas was shot by a sniper "while gallantly leading his men in a successful attack on a strong enemy position".

His Colonel wrote: "*In him we lose a very gallant officer and a dear comrade*". The Chaplain wrote to Thomas' wife, Minnie Ross Stanfield whom he married just a few weeks before he was killed: "*We had all learned to love your husband. He was very popular with officers and men, and his strong, fine character was a great asset to the regiment. I shall not soon forget the last two Sundays. On the first of the two I held a short service in camp, and your husband stood by my side singing very heartily. On the second Sunday I stood by his side under the stars and laid him to rest. It was a sad privilege to do this last service for him.*" Another officer described his: "*manly, steadfast courage: his kindly, earnest character: and his general efficiency as a brave a gallant officer*".

A re-constructed trench on the battlefield seen by pupils and staff on their visit to Thiepval Wood on the Somme with the Custodian from Ulster Tower

Frederick James Steele

DoB: October 30 1888

Regt: Dorset attached Royal Berkshire

CGS: 1901-4

DoD: October 13 1915

Age: 26

Commemorated: Loos Memorial, France

Frederick was the third son of David and Annie Steele. In 1901 David Steele was listed as a commercial traveller. Older brothers Herbert and Ernest were working as an assistant librarian and railway clerk respectively.

While at Carlisle Grammar School, Fred had played Rugby for the school and later for Somerset. He was also a good golfer. He was a scholarship boy, and after leaving he became a schoolmaster, being trained at Carlisle Pupil Teachers Centre, London University and at St Mark's College. Fred became an assistant schoolmaster living at Shepton Mallet in Somerset. Later he worked at Hampton Grammar School. After some years as a teacher, Fred joined a firm of motor manufacturers. At the outbreak of war he came home from Syria, where he had been employed as an engineer for a motor manufacturer, and joined up.

Initially he started as a private in the Sportsmen's Battalion, in 1914. This was comprised of volunteers who came from the world of sport or entertainment. Later he transferred upon promotion to the 3rd Battalion of the Dorsetshire Regiment, a training unit that remained in England throughout the war. He was killed while attached to the 8th Battalion Royal Berkshire Regiment. This Battalion moved to France on August 8 1915, landing at Le Havre, for transfer to the 1st Brigade in 1st Division.

Frederick was killed in action at Hulloch, France, during one of the final assaults of the Battle of Loos. This was a bright sunny day and poison gas was used. The 1st Brigade attacked at 2pm and came under heavy fire from the German positions.

The bombardment had failed to cut the wire significantly and the attack was halted. The survivors withdrew after dark and there were 1200 casualties. Overall there were 61,000 casualties sustained in this campaign. Of these 7,766 were killed, including many men who had only been in France a short while.

On October 6, 1915, Fred made his will in Rouen, France, just before he went into action. He wanted a piece of jewellery to be purchased for Miss Gwen Whelan, in the case of his death. After Fred died a letter from his brother Herbert, enquired about his belongings and asked for a reply to his address as: *"my parents are too old and too distraught with grief to carry on any correspondence"*. However in the Cumberland News, his parents thanked *"all friends for their kind messages of sympathy"*.

The illuminated montage showing the missing soldiers of the Somme.
Thiepval Museum

Edgar Marsden Stewardson

DoB: April 13 1891

Regt: Rifle Brigade

CGS: 1905-6

DoD: September 18 1916

Stewardson on the Thiepval Memorial

Age: 25

Commemorated: Thiepval Memorial, France

Edgar was the fourth of eight children born to John Stewardson and Margaret Marsden. The family had humble origins: John was born to Maria Stewardson whilst she was in the Union Workhouse at Ulverston. The boy was then adopted by his maternal grandparents and took his mother's name.
After assisting his father to run the family laundry on Warwick Road, Carlisle, Edgar worked at Brighton, and at the time of enlisting in the Rifle Brigade, was the deputy manager of Messrs Spiers and Pond's laundry in London.

Edgar had been unsuccessful in joining the Border Regiment in Carlisle and another regiment in Brighton. He had been with the 11th Battalion Rifle Brigade (The Prince Consort's Own) since March 1915. On August 22 1916 this Brigade was part of the 20th Light Division commanded by Major General W. Douglas-Smith on the Somme.

The third phase of the Battle of the Somme began on September 15 with an advance along a six mile front. Flers, Martinpuich, Courcelette and High Wood were captured although there was a delay at Les Boeufs. Courcelette was the first time tanks had ever been employed. It seems Edgar was killed in action at Les Boeufs. The Cumberland News of November 11 1916 reported that Edgar's parents had received official notification that their son was missing.

Frederick Noel Tassell

DoB: December 25 1897

Regt: 20th Royal Fusiliers, Public Schools.

CGS: 1912-13

DoD: April 10 1917

Age: 19

Commemorated: Arras Memorial, France

Courtesy Tassell family

Noel was the second of four children born to Frederick William and Gertrude (née Harrison) Tassell. His father was a photographer born at Brighton. His mother was from Mansfield and had been a photographer's assistant. In 1901 the family was living on Devonshire Street, and in 1911, at 16 Warwick Square. Noel was an engineering apprentice at the L. & N.W, Rly. Works,at Crewe. His employment record reveals he had been employed four years five months (not sure how this was possible if he only left school in 1913). His conduct is recorded as "*Good*".

The Cumberland News reported that Private Tassell was wounded by shrapnel in the back and "is *now progressing favourably in hospital at Birmingham*." This was in September 1916. The Roll of Honour from January 6 1917 includes Noel's photograph and he was described as wounded. Whether this was concerning the same injury he sustained in September is unclear.

There was an Allied Offensive at Arras between April 9 and May 4 1917 and he is indeed commemorated at Arras, France. Noel was reported missing at Monchy, April 10, 1917.

Brother Archibald also served in the Great War, having left school in 1915. He was a Private, Edinburgh Univ. O.T.O. After the war he became a photographer.

Harold Vaughan Tattersall

DoB: June 27 1887

Regt: North Staffordshire

CGS: 1898

DoD: April 22 1918

Age: 30

Buried: Berlin South-Western Cemetery, Germany

Harold was born in Barnet, Hertfordshire, the son of Henry V Tattersall, a bank cashier, and his wife, Edith. He had an older sister, also Edith. Harold was admitted to Carlisle Grammar School in April 1898, but it is unclear when he left and moved to Cranleigh. He was also educated at University College, London where he entered the Faculty of Science in 1906. He passed inter. science in 1908 and took his B.Sc. in 1911. He was Vice-President of the Union Society in 1913-14. In December 1913 he was awarded his Rugby colours.

Harold was working as an analytical chemist when he joined the Royal Fusiliers in Westminster on September 15 1914. The following account of Harold's war service comes from UCL records: *"In August 1914, Tattersall applied for a commission and joined the Public School and University Corps. He was gazetted to the 11th North Staffordshire Regiment on November 23, 1914, and served on the Western Front. On March 21, 1918, during the German offensive, he found himself facing heavy odds; he collected a handful of men and was last seen fighting desperately, although seriously wounded."*

The family were informed on April 15 that he was a prisoner of war but also that he was wounded. He died of his wounds, (shot in jaw and oedema of the lungs), as a prisoner in German hands on April 22, 1918. The Cumberland News reported he died when his regiment was engaged in the great German Offensive and that he made *"gallant resistance against the odds."*

Thomas Edward Thomlinson

DoB: June 3 1870

Regt: Remounts Army Service Corps

CGS: 1882-5

DoD: August 8 1917

Age: 47

Loading horses for transport to war.

Buried: Brighton City (Bear Road) Cemetery, United Kingdom

Thomas was the son of John and Emma Thomlinson his father was a landowner and cement manufacturer. The family lived at Englethwaite Hall, Wetheral. In 1884 Thomas was readmitted to Carlisle Grammar School, having been first admitted in 1882. In 1885-6 he went to Repton School.

In 1911 Thomas was working as a journalist in Lambeth. He was 40 years old and married to Ethel May, 33, an actress. They had married in 1901. Ethel had had two children before her marriage Gladys May Thomas and Harley Miricia Thomas, both of whom had the name Thomlinson in the 1911 census.

Thomas has the distinction of being the oldest casualty of the school in the Great War. Clearly he felt he had to contribute and he became a "Rough-rider" for the Remounts Army Service Corps, which was concerned with the finding and breaking of horses suitable for the war. Of course, the cavalry was being used less in front line action, but horses were still in great demand as transport animals moving everything up to the front from water carts to artillery. The men, who worked as rough-riders tended to be older, more experienced soldiers, who had often had experience in the Boer War. This should have been a safe occupation for Thomas - although some horses were unruly - but he was not to see the war to its conclusion. He died at the Eastern Military Hospital, Brighton, of an aneurism and heart failure on August 8 1917.

Percy Langhorn Thompson

DoB: October 16 1886

Regt: DLI

CGS: 1904-6

DoD: June 11 1917

Age: 30

Buried: Philosophe Military Cemetery , Mazingarbe, Bethune, France

Percy was the seventh child and fourth son of Robert Thompson and Jane Ann Langhorn. His father was an accountant. Percy was in the school cricket team in 1904 and 1905; the Rugby team in 1904 and 1905; and football team in 1906.

After leaving school he trained as a solicitor.Percy enlisted as a private in the 17th Middlesex Battalion (Public Schools Battalion) on April 30 1915. He travelled to France from Folkestone on April 22 1916. He was in Etaples until May 4 when he joined a French mortar battalion. On October 19 1916 he was sent back to England to join the Officer Cadet Unit. He joined the battalion at Oxford on December 1 1916. He was later gazetted (April 25 1917) as a 2nd Lieutenant in the Durham Light Infantry.

In June 1917 the Durham Light Infantry was holding the line at Loos between Boyau 51 to Cameron Alley. A Coy Right Front, C Coy Left Front, B Coy in the village line and D Coy in Reserve battalion HQ at Tosh Keep. Percy Thompson was recorded as killed in action on June 11 1917, during the tour of duty in the trenches between June 9 and 18. While his death is listed in the War Battalion Diary, the specific cause was not given. There was a raid during this time on German trenches on June 15 but he was reported killed by this time. There were patrols out before this so that is a possible reason but if so, it would perhaps have been stated as he was a 2nd Lieutenant.

Harold Vincent Tiffen

DoB: November 10 1894

Regt: Lancashire Fusiliers

CGS: 1905-10

DoD: November 20 1917

Age: 23

Commemorated: Thiepval Memorial, France

Harold was the elder son of James Tiffen and Catherine (née Findley). On his mother's side the family came from Scotland. The Tiffen side were Cumbrian for generations. James was a draper on Scotch Street and Warwick Road.
Harold attended the Grammar School for five years and he was a keen member of the cricket team. He then attended Grosvenor College, Carlisle and became a dental student for a year with John Keswick.

He enlisted in the Royal Army Medical Corps as a private and he went to France in 1915. On being promoted to 2nd Lieutenant in September 1917 he joined the Lancashire Fusiliers. He was last seen two months later on November 20 1917 entering a German trench with his men. In his obituary in the Cumberland News a letter written to his father by the Major commanding the Lancashire Fusiliers is quoted:

"In the attack your son led his men gallantly and his bravery was an example to us all. He proved himself a fine and fearless soldier and a splendid leader. During the short time your son was with this battalion he made many friends, and we that are left cherish a memory of one we are proud of. Please accept our deepest sympathy in your great anxiety and trouble" another letter quoted said *"He was a brave boy and had the makings of a really good officer"*

Thomas Henry Tiffin

DoB: May 29 1893

Regt: Border

CGS: 1905-11

DoD: July 15 1916

Age: 23

Commemorated: Thiepval Memorial, France

Thomas was the youngest son of four born to Thomas Tiffin and his wife Elizabeth (née Mattinson). Thomas was a "relieving officer". Thomas and Elizabeth's families came from the Caldbeck area.
Thomas attended the Grammar School as a day pupil before going to Chester Training College, to train to be a teacher. At school Thomas was a great sportsman; he won prizes for cricket ball throwing, high jump, broad jump, and played for the cricket, Rugby and football teams and won the half mile running race and the 300 yard dash. He really shone on the cricket field where he was a good bowler and was described in *"The Carliol"* magazine as *"a natural bat with a wonderful stroke to leg".*

Thomas joined the 8th Battalion of the Border Regt as a private, but the exact date of his enlistment is unknown. The battalion wasn't mobilised for war until September 27 1915. July 1916 was a costly month for the battalion because on the 2/3 July nearly 450 of their number were killed at Martinsaart Wood near Thiepval. They then had a week in the reserve line of trenches. Between July 8 and 12 the battalion was gradually deployed to the front line. On July 13 and 14 they attacked the German line at Ovillers. Thomas died on July 15, the day the Cheshire Regt relieved them.

Maurice George Trousdell

Dob: December 16 1883

Regt: RASC

CGS: 1894-1900

DoD: August 6 1917

Age: 33

Buried: Canada Farm Cemetery, Belgium

Courtesy of Trousdell family

Maurice was one of 15 children born to Captain William Blakeney Persse Trousdell and his wife Ellen Philippa Louisa Whatman. Captain Trousdell was a retired cavalry officer, landowner and farmer. Three of Maurice's brothers also attended Carlisle Grammar School. Maurice came to the Grammar School on a scholarship and played in the school's Rugby team in 1899 and the cricket team in 1900.

All four brothers served during the Great War: Hugh and Charles were in Nigeria; John in India; and Maurice was fighting in Belgium. Hugh was drowned in 1915 when the ship, *SS Falaba*, he was travelling on, was torpedoed. (See entry on WHC Trousdell)

Maurice left school at the age of 17 to go into Lloyd's Bank. He was in a London branch first, and was then transferred to Maidstone in 1901. The following year he joined the Standard Bank of South Africa, and went to Cape Town in May 1902. While in Cape Town he took a great interest in rowing, and was one of the East London crew who won the Colonial Cup at the first Zambesi Regatta, in June, 1905. After six years in South Africa he came home for three months leave, went out again and was in Nairobi when war broke out. Maurice was originally commissioned into the 2nd Volunteer Battalion of the Queen' Own Royal West Kent Regiment on January 2 1901. He was then re-commissioned on May 4 1915 into "Our Land Forces" as a 2nd Lieutenant.

Maurice joined the Royal Army Service Corps and was appointed a Lieutenant in the 436th Company of the Guards Division Train. This Company was responsible for bringing supplies by rail from the ports to an advanced supply depot and transferring the supplies onto the front. He went to France with the Train on August 21 1915. In 1917, by then a captain, he was stationed at the Advanced Supply Depot at International Corner, near Eykhock in Belgium, organising the shipment of supplies from trains to lorries for the front. On August 6 1917 a German aeroplane dropped a bomb – a rare event – on the depot killing Maurice, wounding another officer and two servicemen, one of whom died later from his wounds.

The following is an extract from a letter from Major Landon, A.S.C., Guards Divisional Train: - *"He was mortally wounded at 3 p.m. of August 6th by a bomb, and Captain Estall and two men were at the same time very dangerously wounded. It will be a great relief to you all to know that he suffered no pain; he lived for twenty minutes, and for the first ten was fully conscious; his only remarks were, "I am afraid that I am badly hit," and then, "How is poor old Estall?" ...he took (some brandy) saying, "I am not in pain." He then became unconscious, and passed away peacefully almost immediately. He was buried at ten a.m. on August 7th, at Canada Farm Military Cemetery......Your son's death has caused us all the greatest grief, for he was most popular, and had been with us since the formation of the Train. He and I have been intimately acquainted in our work for the last two years, and I cannot tell you with what admiration and respect I always regarded him. I think that he was one of the very finest specimens of manhood in every way that I have ever met, and I realise that in him I have lost a most loyal and genuine friend, and the service the most hard working, conscientious and unselfish officer, who never spared himself where the welfare of the troops was concerned. I do not know if you are aware that since he has been in France his name has twice been forwarded for recognition...."*

William Hugh Cornwallis Trousdell

DoB: January 9 1879

CGS: 1893 - 98

DoD: March 28 1915

Age: 36

Hugh was renowned for his cricketing abilities while at school, and was captain of the team. He was also in the Rugby team. He was awarded prizes in French, Greek testament and arithmetic. He was a prefect. He went on to read history at Oxford. At Queen's, Hugh had an interview with the Provost who recorded notes on him: ' *...healthy & strong, played cricket & a little football, hockey, intends to row, fishes & shoots, cannot sing or play, debated & national history society, hopes to get into Civil Service...*" Hugh played hockey at University. While at Oxford the South African War broke out and he at once joined the University Volunteers and went with them to South Africa.

Hugh then joined the Colonial Service in West Africa and was appointed a clerk in the Colonial Audit Department in 1904. He was in the Colonial Civil Service in Northern Nigeria for 11 years and was chief accountant of the Nigerian Railways. Having been invalided home from West Africa in 1914, Hugh was returning to Northern Nigeria in 1915, when his passenger ship the *S.S. Falaba* was torpedoed in the Bristol Channel by a German submarine. He apparently saved all his official papers by throwing them into a boat, but he lost his own life. Hugh was one of the 104 people who drowned. It was the first sinking of a passenger ship of the war and caused outrage in neutral USA as one of the dead was an American engineer, the first American to be killed in the war. The sinking of the *S.S.Falaba* remains controversial.

At the time of his death Hugh was engaged to Sybyl Thesiger, the sister of the explorer and author Wilfred Thesiger and granddaughter of Lord Chelmsford (Anglo-Zulu War). At his Memorial Service, Hugh was described as: *"a Christian, an Englishman and a Gentleman".*

Thomas Mashiter Tyson

DoB: June 10 1898

RFC: 121 Squadron

CGS: 1911-16

DoD: June 12 1918

Age: 20

Buried: Narborough All Saints Churchyard, Norfolk,UK

Thomas Mashiter Tyson was the only child of Thomas Tyson and Minnie Barber and was born in Liverpool. His father was an engineer surveyor from Ulverston, the son of a grocer, and his mother was the daughter of shopkeepers from High Leigh, Cheshire. The name Mashiter was the maiden name of his paternal grandmother. While at school, Thomas was reputed to be a good swimmer and was in the Rugby team: *"useful in the scrum"* and in 1913 won a prize for drawing.

During the Great War, Thomas was a cadet in the RAF and had taken his certificate on a Graham-White Biplane at Hendon on 4 May 1918. He was killed at Narborough Airfield in Norfolk. At 6.30am Thomas had taken up an aircraft assigned to the Americans based there. It was a rebuilt Armstrong Whitworth FK3 (B8827). According to the subsequent court of enquiry Thomas was neither experienced nor qualified enough to fly this aeroplane solo. He had no orders to do so. He stalled the machine shortly after take-off and as he turned, the aeroplane nosedived into the ground from a height of some 50 feet and caught fire. Thomas was pinned by his feet. Lieut EB Humphries and A/Cpl OC Meckel, rushed into the flames in a brave attempt to save him. A fire engine arrived and Thomas was pulled from the burning plane. His commanding officer later commended the two men for their *"great presence of mind and courage".* A telegram was immediately sent to his parents to *"come at once"* as their son had been seriously injured. This was followed up by a second telegram an hour later to report that Thomas had died: without regaining consciousness. The Inventory of his belongings contains everything from the most mundane (a pair slippers; eight pairs socks etc) to some items that give clues about his interests (13 pieces of music; six novels; one vest pocket Auto camera; three pipes and a tin of tobacco).

Thomas' father later complained about the cost of his travel from Carlisle (£6 5s) which he had paid - it had not been explained that he could apply to the nearest Police Station in case of difficulty - for fear of offending him.

The Narborough Local History Society unveiled a memorial plaque to those who served at Narborough in 1998. In September 2011 a new memorial was unveiled to mark the airfield and commemorate the 41 men who were killed there. A Tornado made a fly past and RAF Marham supplied a guard of honour. In his book on the airfield, David Turner described Thomas so: *"a typical young flier, perhaps, for whom the thrill of flying solo proved impossible to resist. A moment's impulsiveness cost him his life".* He was just 20 years and two days old.

Courtesy of David Ramshaw

A small British cemetery on a hill near Thiepval

Thomas Sidney Wathes

DoB: November 2 1887

Regt: Royal Warwickshire

CGS: 1904-06

DoD: July 19 1916

Age: 28

Commemorated: Ploegsteert Memorial, Belgium

Courtesy of Wathe family

Buried: now believed to be one of those buried in the new cemetery at Fromelles, France

Thomas was the fourth child of Charles Weetman Wathes, a dairyman from Leicestershire, and Caroline, from Warwick.
Thomas was a prefect at school and was secretary of the games committee. He went up to Oxford,: *"Wathes, at Wadham, spends his leisure hours reading History on the river toggering [sic]. He recently made a startling appearance at the Jesus Smoker and may be the cause of the disappearance of several name plates. But stop – not a word!!"* Thomas rowed for the College as bow in the first eight and on going down in 1909 he became a master at King Edward VI, Aston, Birmingham. Thomas married Doris Collins on June 4 1913, and a son, Richard Sidney was born on August 10 1915. Doris was also a graduate of Wadham College.

Captain Wathes fought at Fromelles; a battle begun 19 days after the opening of the Somme campaign further south, and was largely fought by Australian 5th Division. The British units were relatively inexperienced. The attack was a complete military failure according to the war diary. *"immediately they left the trenches the enemy shelled very heavily with the result that in a very short time all the officers had been killed or wounded...two platoons reached the enemy's parapet but owing to the heavy losses caused and the casualties among the officers the attack was unable to advance... Telephone communication with the front line now broke down but in spite of the heavy fire was quickly resolved. Immediately after orders were received that the attack would be postponed... and the survivors would be withdrawn under cover of a barrage by our artillery on the WICK. At 7.10 the barrage started and all who could returned to the trenches. The attack was now postponed till 9.0 pm and later orders were received that the attack would be abandoned...The conduct of all ranks through-out the whole action was most excellent, orders being cheerfully carried out without the slightest hesitation under the most trying conditions.*

Casualties sustained during action fought on 19.7.16 – officers killed Capt W SIMMS – missing...Capt TS WATHES...Other ranks killed 9, missing 68, wounded 154...” (War Diary)

By the time the action was called off the next morning, the Australians had lost 5,513 men killed, wounded and missing. Casualties for the British who attacked alongside the Australians, numbered 1,547.

Many of those killed could not be accounted for at the time, including Thomas. In May 2009 work to recover the dead for individual reburial in a new military cemetery at Fromelles began.

In a BBC news article from July 19 2010, a last letter from a Thomas Sidney Wharfs (sic) on July 18 1916 is quoted thus: *“My darling wife I am writing this to be sent to you in case anything happens and I am killed tonight. I have just been ordered to attack tomorrow and I'm taking my company over, in the front line.*

I am absolutely confident of my men and we'll get through, all correctly but we're certain to have casualties. Cheer up and take care of Dick. You will need all your strength to bring him up and look after him. God bless you my darling wife and boy. I love you with all my heart.”

It is probable this letter was from Thomas Wathes to Doris who was to die just five years later in 1921.

George Trevor Williams

DoB: October 19 1888

Regt: Royal Field Artillery

CGS: 1901 - 06

DoD: April 19 1918

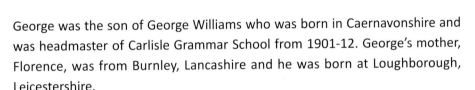

Age: 29

Buried: Rawalpindi War Cemetery, Pakistan

George was the son of George Williams who was born in Caernavonshire and was headmaster of Carlisle Grammar School from 1901-12. George's mother, Florence, was from Burnley, Lancashire and he was born at Loughborough, Leicestershire.

In the 1911 census when George was 22, he was a boarder at an address in Newcastle-upon-Tyne and employed as an engineering draughtsman.

George was commissioned into the Royal Field Artillery on October 13 1914, served in France (1914-15), at Gallipoli (1915), in Egypt (1916), in Mesopotamia (1916) and in India (1916-18). He died in hospital at Rawalpindi, then India, as a result of a fractured skull in April 1918. He was not on duty at the time of the accident. Exactly what caused this is not stated in the report of his death.

Courtesy of David Ramshaw

Growing flax where there were trenches - Hope for the future.

Robert Dixon Wills

DoB: August 6 1893

Regt: Border

CGS: 1905-7

DoD: April 23 1917

Age: 23

Wancourt Mlilitary Cemetery, France

Buried: Wancourt Military Cemetery, France

Robert Dixon Wills was the youngest of ten children born to Isaac and Jane Wills of Greenspot near Kirkbride. Isaac was the village blacksmith, like his father and grandfather before him. Two of Robert's brothers, and at least one cousin and uncle were also blacksmiths. Robert was the only one of the family to attend the Grammar School.

After leaving school Robert went to London and entered the Civil Service as a boy clerk in 1909. By 1914 he was in the Architect's Department of London County Council.

War was declared in August 1914 and Robert volunteered on September 1 1914. As he enlisted in London he joined a London Regiment. He must have impressed those around him as he rose rapidly through the ranks and by the summer of 1916 he was a corporal. He was so proficient in bayonet fighting that he was made an instructor. He was sent to Ireland in early 1916 and to France on June 21 1916.

On August 8 1916 Robert was part of a raiding party, which was sent across no-man's land to raid the German trenches and secure prisoners. The raid was not a success as although the wire had been broken by mortars, the trench itself was barricaded. Most of the party withdrew but Robert managed to crawl under the barricade, secure a prisoner and return with him! As they withdrew they were bombarded by mortars. His commanding officer was wounded and had to take refuge in a shell hole with another wounded man. In his commanding officer's report he says this about Robert:

"This man was very plucky throughout the whole raid and I should like to bring his name to your notice"

The Cumberland News describes the incident too *"He (Robert) formed one of the party which raided the trenches of the enemy on a certain night. While returning to our trenches he lost his way and his rifle was smashed by a trench motar bomb. Finding himself close to a German trench, he entered it unarmed, rushed an armed German sentry and brought him back to our lines. He also took charge of two of our wounded men who had lost their way"*

Robert was awarded the Military Medal on September 21, and was sent to cadet school for a commission in October. He was commissioned as an officer and chose to be posted to the 5th Border Regiment on Dec 22 1916.

The Border Regiment was involved in heavy fighting at Wancourt on April 23/24 1917 when 74 men were killed or missing in action and 135 were wounded; Robert was one of the six officers who died. He was buried in a marked grave and after the war his body was exhumed and reburied in Wancourt Military Cemetery.

His obituary in the Cumberland News includes an extract of a letter sent to Robert's sister by one of his comrades Second Lieutenant James Thompson:

"It is with the deepest regret that I have to inform you of the death in action of Second Lieutenant R. D. Wills. He was instantaneously killed by shrapnel just previous to the battalion advancing to the assault. I have known him intimately since he first joined us, and can assure you no officer was better loved and respected by everyone from the C.O. downwards, than he was. His body was brought back to a cemetery in a village near where he fell. A service was held by a clergyman and he was interred alongside three brother officers, who fell on the same day". Further on the obituary it says *"Lieutenant Wills was a man of fine physique, and on more than one occasion his knowledge of Cumberland wrestling stood him in good stead in hand to hand encounters with the enemy, and in raids, etc."*

William James Wilson

DoB: May 27 1894

Regt: Devonshire

CGS: 1907-11

DoD: April 25 1917

Age: 22

Courtesy Richard Preston

Commemorated: Doiran Memorial, Greece

William was the third son of William James Wilson and Amelia Challenger. His father was a shopkeeper by 1911 and had been a loco engine stoker, son of a coach smith.
After leaving the Grammar School, William became a student teacher at Robert Ferguson School, Carlisle.

The Allies had a presence in northern Greece from October 1915 when a combined Franco-British force of two large brigades landed at Salonika (today Thessalonika) to support the Serbs against the Bulgarians. By the time they arrived – at the request of the Greek Prime Minister – the Serbs had already been defeated but the Salonika force dug in despite the opposition of some Greeks. This became an International Force as in 1916 the troops were joined by Russian, Italian and Serbian soldiers. This prevented an invasion of Greece by Bulgaria.

As William was killed on April 25 1917 it seems probable he died during the First Battle of Doiran which took place between April 22 and May 8 1917. Conditions in the region were appalling and more men died of sickness than in engaging the enemy, although William was killed in action.

William Ewart Gladstone Wise

DoB: April 24 1894

Regt: Royal Field Artillery

CGS: 1907-9

DoD: October 29 1916

Age: 25

Buried: Courcelette Cemetery, France

William Ewart Gladstone served four terms as Liberal Prime Minister; his final term ending in 1894, the year Willliam Wise was born. His father may have been a farm labourer and dock labourer at Causewayhead, Silloth, but his political affiliations were clear. William the youngest of six children won a scholarship to the Grammar School. He was in the school's Rugby team and worked for his father after he left school. He was a keen Silloth Rugby player.
When William enlisted and became a gunner, the teachers and choir of St Paul's, Causeway Head presented him with a wristlet watch as a token of their esteem.

He was reported as being killed in action on the Somme in October 1916. The Battle of the Somme lasted nearly five months and involved several distinct actions. The Battle of Flers-Courcelette took place in September 1916. The Battle of Ancre Heights was going on at the time William was killed. These campaigns were all part of the Somme's "Big Push".

The Cumberland News reported that the officer under whom "Gladdy Wise" had served said: *"He was killed instantaneously when in action on the gun by an enemy shell. He had been the battery signaller for a long time, and a very good one too, and we shall be the poorer for his loss. I had offered him promotion quite recently, but he did not want it."*

Francis Noel Wright

DoB: November 12 1891

Regt: King's Liverpool

CGS: 1903-7

DoD: September 17 1917

Age: 25

Buried: White House Cemetery, St.Jean-les -Ypres, Belgium

Francis was the youngest of five children of William Ingle Wright, a commercial clerk in a printing works and Eliza Margaret Edmiston. He was born in Carlisle. His father, and Francis's four older siblings Margaret, Alice, Robert, and William were all born in Suffolk.

Francis's mother came from Montserrat, West Indies. Her father Robert born in Glasgow died in Montserrat. In 1881 and 1891 Eliza's mother Sarah Hyde was living at The Friends Retreat Lunatic Asylum, Walmgate, York and listed as a lady's companion and an officer and a widow.

In 1911 Francis was an apprentice printer. He enlisted in Liverpool. In September 1917 the Liverpool Regiment was largely in billets undergoing training. There was even a divisional horse show on September 6. On September 15 the battalion moved from Zutkerque to Vlamertinghe outside Ypres and to *'Mersey Camp to view the model of the Zonnebeke area'* on September 16. The War Diary notes that the following day the camp was *"shelled a little - casualties 1 OR (other ranks) died of wounds"*. It seems Francis was very unlucky.

Last Song written on 13 June 1918

Henry Lamont Simpson

All my songs are risen and fled away;
(Only the brave birds stay);
All my beautiful songs are broken or fled.
My poor songs could not stay
Among the filth and the weariness and the dead.

There was bloody grime on their light, white feathery wings,
(Hear how the lark still sings),
And their eyes were the eyes of dead men that I knew.
Only a madman sings
When half of his friends lie asleep for the rain and the dew.

The flowers will grow over the bones of my friends;
(The birds' song never ends);
Winter and summer, their fair flesh turns to clay.
Perhaps before all ends
My songs will come again that have fled away.

Places of Burial and Commemoration

BELGIUM
Canada Farm Cemetery
Maurice George Trousdell
Dranoutre Military Cemetery
Herbert Ronald Farrar
Hooge Crater Cemetery
Walter Henderson
John Mitchell Mackay
Menin Gate
James Robert Caird
Hugh Richard Hyndman-Jones
John Mitchell Lee
Hop Store Cemetery
Arthur Edward Basil Dixon
Ploegsteert Memorial
Robert Clow Foster
Thomas Sidney Wathes
Tyne Cot Memorial
Robert Abram
Charles Cecil Forster
Douglas Ronald Maurice Hannay
Thomas Hindson Mellish
George Norman
William Dalton Columbo Sharp
William Sinclair
White House Cemetery St-Jean-les-Ypres
Francis Noel Wright

CANADA
Mount Pleasant Cemetery, London, Ontario
Beresford Karr Horan

FRANCE
A.I.F. Burial Ground, Flers
George McPherson
Aire Communal Cemetery
Edward Hughes Dodgson
Anneux British Cemetery
Thomas William Stanfield
Arras Memorial
Frederick Noel Tassell
Bailleul Communal Cemetery Ext Nord
Edward Leslie Dixon
Bethune Town Cemetery
Henry Frederick Edgecumbe Edwardes
Bienvillers Military Cemetery
Charles Reeves Liddell
Bray Military Cemetery
John Asheton Critchley
Cambrai Mem Louverval
Bertie Bowman Barton
Cite Bonjean Military Cemetery Armentieres
Reginald John Atkinson
Combles Communal Cemetery Ext
Douglas Alexander Mackay Shepherd
Courcelette British Cemetery
William Ewart Gladstone Wise
Ebblinghem Military Cemetery
Richard Beeby
Favreuil British Cemetery
Charles Bertram Dove
Le Touret
James Herbert Batey
William Stafford Curtis
Bernard Arthur Johnson

Loos Memorial
Robert de Glanville
Frederick James Steele
Norfolk Cemetery Becordel-Becourt
Francis Richard Lowry Bell
Philosophe British Cemetery, Mazingarbe
George Bott
Percy Langhorn Thompson
Pommereuil British Cemetery
James Graham
Pont du Hem Military British Cemetery, La Gorgue
John Santiago Campbell
Pozieres
Arthur Hetherington
John Scott
Quarry Cemetery Montauban
Stanley Campbell Cheverton
Cyril Herbert Le Tall
Ribemont Communal Cemetery Ext Somme
Peter Sydenham Dixon
Serre Road Cemetery No 2
Robert Mayson Calvert
Soissons Memorial
James Dowell Parkin
Ste Marie Cemetery, Le Havre
Harry Scott Higginson
St Sever Cemetery Ext Rouen
Nathaniel George Dobson
Kenneth James Stafford
Sunken Road Cemetery Contalmaison
Joseph Dodd
Thiepval
Huntley William Bruce Bremner
Edward Stanley Curwen
James Whaley Fryer
William Graham
John Morrison Jessamine
William Keir Little

Malcolm Macdonald
Henry Allason Peile
Edgar Marsden Stewardson
Harold Vincent Tiffen
Thomas Henry Tiffin
Vimy Memorial
Lawrence Stanley Carrick
John Dixon
Vis-en-Artois Memorial
Henry Lamont Simpson
Wancourt British Cemetery
Robert Dixon Wills

GERMANY
Berlin South Western Cemetery
Harold Vaughan Tattersall

GREECE
Doiran Memorial
William James Wilson

INDIA
Madras Chennai
Robert James Dixon
Walter Maxwell

IRAQ
Amara War Cemetery
William Joseph Cornwall Laurie
Basra Memorial
Otway Trevor MacRitchie Leckie
Herbert Curry McCumiskey
James Bruce Pearson

ITALY
 Granezza British Cemetery
Eric William Lafone
Montecchio Precalcino Communal Cemetery

Maxwell Ogilvy-Ramsay
Staglieno Cemetery Genoa
James Blackwood Hay

LATVIA
Nikolai Cemetery
Henry Siviour Carruthers

PAKISTAN
Rawalpindi War Cemetery
George Trevor Williams

TURKEY
Helles Memorial
George Newell Ballantine
Richard Parker Gilbanks

UNITED KINGDOM
Brighton City Cemetery (Bear Road)
Thomas Edward Thomlinson
Chatham Naval Memorial
Frank Bousfield Somerville
Narborough (All Saints) Churchyard, Norfolk
Thomas Mashiter Tyson
Rugeley Cemetery
Christopher Edward Parker
Plymouth Naval Memorial
Walter Jackson
Tower Hill Memorial London
William Glaister Irving

ZAMBIA
Ndola Cemetery
Alastair Bruce Bremner

OTHER
William Hugh Cornwallis Trousdell

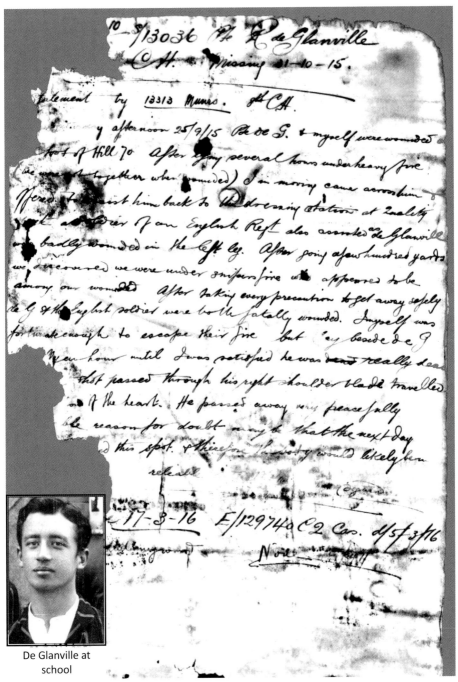

10 - 9/13036 Pte De Glanville
C.H. Missing 21-10-15.

Statement by 13313 Munro. 8th C.A.

... y afternoon 25/9/15 Pte de G. & myself were wounded at foot of Hill 70. After lying several hours under heavy fire (we ... together when wounded) In moving came across him & offered to assist him back to the dressing station at Zuality ... order of an English Regt also assisted as De Glanville ... badly wounded in the left leg. After going a few hundred yards we discovered we were under snipers fire who appeared to be among our wounded. After taking every precaution to get away safely ... G & the English soldier were both fatally wounded. Myself was ... weak enough to escape their fire but ... beside de G ... an hour until I was satisfied he was ... really dead ... shot passed through his right shoulder blade travelled ... of the heart. He passed away very peacefully ... be reason for doubt may be that the next day ... this spot & therefore ... would likely be ... relieved.

De Glanville at school

Private Munro's letter re- De Glanville - See page 54.

1912 Rugby XV - W Graham, B A Johnson, T H Mellish and De Glanville are in this team. It is interesting to note that these photographs were all taken by Carlisle photographer Fred W Tassell, father of Noel Tassell.

Edward Stanley Curwen and colleagues - see page 32.

PRO PATRIA
1914- 1918

IN GRATEFUL MEMORY OF THE OLD CARLIOLS WHO DIED FOR KING AND COUNTRY IN THE GREAT WAR

The full list of the Fallen as recorded on the
Carlisle Grammar School
First World War Memorial which is
situated in the Old Hall,
Upper School building.
(See page 4)

Other local books published by P3 Publications

Title	ISBN	First Published
The Carlisle Ship Canal	978-0-9572412-4-4	October 2013
A Century Around Silloth	978-0-9572412-3-7	October 2012
Chanel &The Tweedmaker	978-0-9572412-2-0	September 2012
Watching Over Carlisle	978-0-9559017-6-8	July 2011
The Cockermouth Floods	978-09559017-3-7	January 2009
The Keswick & Workington Floods	978-09559017-4-4	February 2009
Wetheral & Great Corby	978-09559017-2-0	October 2008
The Carlisle Floods	978-09547739-1-5	January 2005
Carlisle Breweries & Public Houses	978-09547739-0-X	2004

For more books and further details go to
http://www.p3publications.com
Books can be purchased online using Paypal or credit/debit card